Pretty Cakes

The Art of Cake Decorating

∎

MARY GOODBODY
with
JANE STACEY

Pretty Cakes

The Art of Cake Decorating

Contributing Bakers
ELLEN BAUMWOLL
CHERYL KLEINMAN
LISA CATES & JANET ROSS

Photographs by
DAVID ARKY

Illustrations by
NORA HUMPHREY

International Culinary Society
New York

To Laura Wreden Goodbody and Anna Zilke

This 1989 edition published by International Culinary Society, a division of dilithium Press, Ltd., distributed by Crown Publishers, Inc., 225 Park Avenue South, New York, New York 10003.

Produced by Smallwood and Stewart, 9 West 19th Street, New York, N.Y. 10011.

Designed by Bokuniewicz Inc.

Printed and bound in Spain
Artes Gráficas Toledo, S.A.
D.L.TO:2263-1988
ISBN 0-517-677296
hgfedcba

Library of Contress Cataloging in Publication Data

Goodbody, Mary.

  Pretty Cakes.

  Includes index.
  1. Cakes decorating. I. Title

TX771.G63 1986 641.8'653 85-45201

▪ CONTENTS ▪

Introduction

Alert your family and friends: they are about to eat cake. And appreciate it as never before. We set out to write a book about cake decorating, one that would take the art a step beyond other books by focusing on the entire cake—the flavor, texture, and appearance of every element that goes into a beautiful cake (and there are a lot!). We ended up accomplishing that and much more. The book is packed with baking as well as decorating information. Our cakes run from simple to elaborate, and each is carefully planned, designed to appeal to all the senses, to all levels of expertise and taste. Some you will want to make right away, others you may prefer to dream about. But whether you spend almost as much time gazing at the photographs as you do in the kitchen, we hope *Pretty Cakes* will inspire, satisfy, and inform you.

It was no simple task to put this book together. First, we recruited talented bakers who contributed their own special styles. Ellen Baumwoll is a pro who wields a parchment paper cone with the grace of an artist. Her delicate cakes, with their painstakingly intricate designs, are certainly among the most stunning in the book. Cheryl Kleinman uses a pastry bag with daring as well as skill, and molds marzipan and pastillage with cunning and imagination. Frequently flamboyant, her cakes also can be sweetly pretty and demure.

No task is too daunting for Jane Stacey, and it's her generous spirit that infuses virtually every page of this book. Her cakes have a simple elegance, an ease and straightforwardness that will appeal to advanced bakers and yet won't intimidate beginners. Jane also provided the recipes in Chapter 2—clear, concise baking formulas for the cakes, frosting, and fillings that are used throughout the book. And finally, we called on Lisa Cates and Janet Ross to create two special birthday cakes for kids—and the child in all of us.

It's this mix of decorating styles that makes the book unique. All the cakes are lovely, but some will please one reader more than will others. Some are quite difficult, a challenge to even the most jaded amateur decorator, others are easy enough for the novice. All are sure to lend an air of specialness to any celebration, be it a child's birthday party, a small dinner party, or a formal wedding.

We organized the cakes into seven categories. The cakes in Chapter 3 and 4 are seasonal. The spring and summer cakes are generally light and easy and call for lots of fresh fruit and whipped cream. The fall and winter cakes tend to be a bit more elegant, use more chocolate and nuts, caramel, and marzipan. The final four chapters are self explanatory: cakes for adult and juvenile birthdays, cakes for holidays and special occasions, and finally, wedding, anniversary, and shower cakes.

Putting this book together was a joy, a challenge, and a treat. I am excited about it; I hope you will be too. And now I must get back to the kitchen to finish my mother's birthday cake.

Mary Goodbody

CHAPTER ONE

•

*Ingredients,
Equipment &
Techniques*

Cakes, of course, are served at celebrations, at some they are themselves stars, as with weddings, special birthdays and other milestones; for holidays both solemn and gay; for formal and casual entertaining; and especially for the family at Sunday supper. Though all our cakes are special, many can be assembled and decorated in less than an hour, and a few will require an afternoon or more to finish. Some are decorated with classic techniques, while others are far from traditional. And that's the point. We think decorating a cake provides an avenue for visual creativity that is perhaps lacking in the other courses of the meal.

That isn't to say there are no rules. Just as you must understand the basic premises of cake baking and frosting to make a moist, tender cake with a flawless creamy frosting, you must master the correct way to fill and hold a pastry bag, to roll marzipan and fondant, and to make chocolate curls and ribbons. You will learn all these techniques and more in this book. Once you have acquired the techniques, there are few boundaries. Use your imagination. Succumb to whim. Recreate these cakes, or use them as inspiration for your own.

We take the entire cake into account when we decorate—its texture, flavor, size, filling, and frosting. Sometimes we use the cake itself as the decorating element. The cake may be nothing more exotic than yellow layer cake with chocolate frosting, but may be unusually shaped and garnished with an inventive candle design or a simple arrangement of fruits. At the other end of the spectrum are the classic cakes that require such involved techniques as beveling, smoothing marzipan, and then decorating with a dotted Swiss pattern of piped royal icing and a centerpiece of pastillage flowers.

In Chapter 2 the basic components of decorated cakes—the cakes, fillings, frosting, and decorations—are presented. All the cakes in this book have been developed with these recipes, but you can certainly substitute any family favorite that is appropriate in size and texture.

You will find some cakes that are designed for a beginner and some that should be baked only by an experienced baker. At the beginning of each recipe we indicate its degree of difficulty and tell you about its preparation and the equipment you will need. A work plan tells at a glance how long to allow for baking and preparation, assembly and decoration, and recommends a manageable plan.

Ingredients

Making even the simplest cake will take a couple hours of your time, and so they deserve the highest-quality ingredients for the best flavor and texture. Equally important is working with the correct ingredients, and avoiding risky substitutions.

The Basics

For all our recipes use sweet (unsalted) butter, which tends to be fresher than salted butter and won't upset the balance of a delicate recipe by adding even a minuscule amount of extra salt. For the recipes that follow, have all-purpose flour and large Grade A eggs. Use regular, granulated sugar unless otherwise indicated—as, for example, in the frosting recipe that depends on confectioners' sugar for a smooth, creamy texture.

Always use pure vanilla extract or the seeds from a vanilla bean. Imitation vanilla tastes bland and artificial. Most cake recipes call for baking powder: because humidity reduces its effectiveness, make sure it's less than a year old and has been stored in an airtight container. If you're an occasional baker, date the baking powder can when you open it.

Heavy cream has a slightly higher butterfat content than whipping light cream. Where *heavy* and *whipping* cream are not synonyms for the same product, buy heavy cream.

Chocolate

From the many kinds of chocolate available today, a considered choice will repay your desserts with the rich, honest flavor and texture of real chocolate. Avoid chocolate emulsified with vegetable shortening rather then with cocoa butter, which increases its shelf life but diminishes its taste. Read the label or choose chocolate by brand (Lindt and Tobler both make high-quality chocolates, but there are many others). Price is another indication of quality. It's the cocoa butter and extra refining as well as the top-grade cocoa beans in good chocolate that raise its price, but the richer flavor is worth it. When melting chocolate set it in an uncovered bowl or the top of a double boiler over hot water, being careful not to get any steam or water in it.

Cocoa

For the recipes in this book, use only unsweetened cocoa, preferably Dutch processed, which is less bitter and dissolves more easily in water.

Fruits

Many of our cakes use fresh and dried fruits for their flavor, texture, and appearance. Fresh fruit should be at the height of ripeness. Dried fruits, featured in many of the Fall & Winter cakes, allow for more flexibility, as they will keep well at room temperature for several months, and for up to a year in the refrigerator.

Grapefruit, Lemon, and Orange Peel

Wispy, colorful strips of candied citrus peel bring a delicate dimension to a cake. It's important to use only the zest—the colored outer layer of the fruit—not the whole peel, which includes the bitter white pith. A swivel-type vegetable peeler or small, sharp paring knife will remove peel efficiently. The easiest way to grate zest is with an old-fashioned lemon zester, but if you can't find this useful gadget, a fine grater will work.

Nuts

Buy the freshest nuts possible, preferably in a store where they are sold loose, in bulk. As they can turn rancid very quickly, keep them in the freezer. If you need ground nuts, buy whole ones and grind them in a nut grinder, food processor, or blender, being careful not to overgrind them. Hazelnuts need to be skinned before being ground or chopped, as their skins tend to be tough or bitter. To remove the skins, either blanch the nuts in boiling water with a little baking soda (1 tablespoon for every cup of water) for about 3 minutes; or brown them, spread out on a baking sheet, in a 350° oven for 10 to 15 minutes. The skins should slip off easily when the nuts are rubbed gently in a kitchen towel.

Preserves

We recommend, rather than sweeter jams or jellies, fruit preserves for fillings and glazes in these cakes. With delicate cakes such as genoise, the preserves should be heated and strained to remove pieces of fruit or seeds. With heavier textured cakes such as pound cake and fruitcake, the preserves need not be heated or strained and may be slathered on as filling or frosting for a casual, earthy flavor and texture.

Liqueurs

A little liqueur in a cake or frosting can transform a good cake into a great cake. Liqueur adds a subtle flavor, and it enhances the flavor of other ingredients as well. A sprinkling of liqueur on each layer also helps keep a cake moist. In most cases we've chosen a particular liqueur to complement another ingredient. For example, Framboise is paired with a cake that is filled with fresh raspberries; Grand Marnier or Cointreau in an orange genoise or layer cake. Rum and cognac are both excellent in chocolate cakes and frostings.

Equipment

The right equipment makes cake baking more pleasurable. However, even if you don't have a kitchen stocked with copper bowls and stacks of cake pans, you can still make delicious, beautiful cakes with a modest inventory.

Mixers

A heavy-duty electric mixer with an attached bowl will be enormously helpful for these recipes. A hand-held mixer can be used for some recipes but may not be powerful enough to handle stiff mixtures such as pastillage. If your mixer has both a flat beater and a balloon whisk, use the flat beater for general mixing and the whisk when you need to get as much air as possible into the mixture, as with egg whites.

Ovens

Most home kitchens are equipped with the standard "roasting" oven. Whether it is gas or electric, the intensity of the heat varies according to shelf height, and it's usually best to bake with the rack in the middle position where the heat is most even.

Pans

We have developed these recipes for standard cake pans and home kitchen appliances. Generally you'll need two 8-inch round layer pans. If a recipe calls for a jelly roll pan, the size should be 11½ by 15½ inches. Some cakes are baked in smaller or larger round pans, ranging from 6 to 14 inches, and others are baked in square or rectangular pans, and even stainless steel bowls.

Decorating Equipment

For piping decorations on a cake, a turntable increases your control and helps to produce a uniform design. With the cake centered on the turntable, you can rotate it smoothly while spreading frosting or piping intricate decorations. Two types of turntables are available: a lightweight, two-piece model that is perfectly adequate for the occasional decorator, and a heavy-duty turntable that will support large wedding cakes. But, turntables are not essential for every cake, and in recipes for which they are required, we've indicated them. Cardboard cake rounds allow you to hold the cake in the palm of your hand while applying frosting or decoration, and to transfer the cake efficiently from work surface or turntable to refrigerator to serving plate.

Pastry bags are made of canvas and sometimes lined with plastic, or nylon. Nylon bags are lightweight and pliable but can be slippery. An 8- to 12-inch bag is about right for most cake decorating, and we recommend you have several on hand, especially for cakes with more than one color frosting.

Small decorating tips are numbered according to size and come in various shapes for piping leaves, roses, star borders, rosettes, and other decorations. The Ateco kit containing about twenty-eight tips is inexpensive and has all you need for most of our recipes. With most brands of decorating tips, the numbers are consistent with the shape of the tip. The tips attach to the pastry bag with a plastic coupler, so they can be changed swiftly without removing the frosting from the bag. You will also need two or three large, or standard, plain, round, and star tips that fit directly into the bag, without a coupler. Larger than decorating tips, their fancier variations are noted by a letter, for example, a #5B star tip pipes a more intricate design than an ordinary #5 star tip.

Standard bakers' equipment, metal flower nails in various sizes are used to build up buttercream roses and other flowers petal by petal.

A baker's comb is a decorating tool that scores fine parallel lines on frosting. It is triangle-shaped, with different-sized teeth on each side. Cutters and presses in various shapes—flowers, leaves, birds, animals, stars and many more—and sizes allow a cake decorator to create the most imaginative designs, working with marzipan, pastillage, or fondant. Available at bakers' supply stores, many interesting ones are also carried by ceramic supply stores.

Baker's Equipment

Electric mixer, preferably heavy-duty

Mixing bowls

Measuring cups, both liquid and dry

Measuring spoons

Wooden spoons

Wire whisks

Rubber spatula

Metal cake spatula

Metal pastry scraper

Fine sieve

Sifter

Pastry brushes

Long serrated knife

Paring knife

Oven thermometer

Candy thermometer

Rolling pin

Kitchen timer

Small heavy bottom saucepan

Double boiler

Flat, heavy baking sheets

Wire racks

Parchment paper

Cardboard rounds

Cake dome

Techniques

The baking and decorating techniques that follow may be applied to just about any cake you will ever make. While specific techniques accompany the individual recipes, these general instructions almost always apply as well.

Working with Dry Ingredients, Eggs, and Butter

The measurements given for dry ingredients in our recipes are in cups and spoons. For accuracy, use the "dip-and-sweep" method: dip the cup or spoon into the flour or sugar, and level it by sweeping off the excess with a knife. When the recipe reads "1 cup of flour, sifted" measure the flour, then sift. Conversely "1 cup of sifted flour" indicates the flour should be sifted first, then measured. Be sure to fold sifted flour thoroughly into the batter with swift, light strokes, as pockets of unincorporated flour form hard lumps during baking.

Separate eggs when they are cold, but for maximum volume, bring them to room temperature before beating the whites or yolks. When you are beating egg whites, make sure both bowl and beaters are clean; grease or a bit of egg yolk will inhibit their expansion to maximum volume.

Butter should always be at room temperature before you beat it to a pale yellow color and creamy, fluffy consistency. It usually takes one to two minutes with an electric mixer to reach this stage, but the exact time depends on the quantity, and the general temperature and humidity of your kitchen. In winter, for instance, when room temperature is normally cooler than in summer, you'll need to allow a little more time to cream the butter. Cream butter with a paddle attachment if your beater has one.

Stirring, Beating, Whisking, and Folding

When a recipe specifies stirring, this should be done by hand with a wooden spoon or rubber spatula. Beating and whisking may be done with an electric mixer. It's a little easier to cream butter with a flat beater, if your mixer has one; otherwise the whisk attachment is fine for creaming, as well as for whisking eggs or cream.

Folding is a fundamental technique for incorporating a fragile ingredient, such as beaten egg whites or whipped cream, into a mixture without deflating it in the process. Always fold with a rubber spatula to add the delicate ingredient into the rest of the batter or mixture gradually rather than all in one dollop.

To fold, spoon about a quarter or a third of the beaten egg whites (or whipped cream) onto the mixture in the bowl. Cut the spatula vertically into the center of the batter and then bring it across the bottom of the bowl, up one side, and back to the center so that part of the fragile ingredient is incorporated. Repeat this movement, bringing the spatula up the other side of the bowl. Continue the process, moving the spatula first to one side of the bowl and then to the other, until both elements are incorporated, without any loss of volume. Work swiftly but gently.

When a recipe calls for beaten or whipped egg whites or cream, be sure to beat to the stage specified in the recipe. Stiff peaks should retain their shape when you lift the beaters off them; soft peaks have volume but will gradually fall back into themselves, at least partially, when you stop beating.

Add liquid and dry ingredients to a cake batter alternately, beginning and ending with the dry ingredients and scraping down the sides of the bowl as you do so. Your main aim with this step is to blend the ingredients smoothly without overworking the batter. It's best to do this by hand with a rubber spatula, as this gives you more control. Poorly or hastily mixed batter results in a cake with an uneven crumb or a heavy texture.

Baking and Cooling the Cake

Most of our recipes tell you to butter and flour pans before filling, rather than lining them with waxed or parchment paper. Use a light but thorough touch with the butter being sure to cover the sides and reach the corners—and a mere dusting of flour, shaking off any excess.

The length of baking time is specified in each recipe but the exact time depends on your oven temperature—and every oven is different. Consider the time given only as a guide in each recipe and rely on doneness tests to determine exactly when to remove the cake from the oven. Pierce the cake at the center (not near the side unless specified) with a toothpick or fine skewer; if it comes out clean, the cake is done. The cake will also pull away slightly from the sides of the pan when it is done and will spring back when lightly touched with a fingertip.

Cakes should be cooled to slightly warm before they are turned out of their pans. Set the pans on wire racks or inverted bowls or glasses so that air can circulate freely all around them.

To turn a cooled cake out onto a turntable, cardboard round, or flat serving plate, run a metal spatula or thin-bladed knife around the sides of the cake to loosen it, then invert. The cardboard round should be the same size as the cake, or, if the frosting will be thick, about a half-inch wider. If the cake has cooled so much that it's hard to get out of the pan, return it to the oven for a minute or two.

Preparing a Cake for Frosting

To slice a cake into layers, place it on a turntable or cardboard round, and with the palm of your hand flat on top of the cake, turn the cake carefully against the serrated blade of a long knife, making a slight sawing motion with the knife. Turn until the cake is cut all around, about one inch in, and then repeat the motion until the cake is cut through. Never try to pick up thin cake layers with your hands; use a cardboard round or baking sheet for support.

Before frosting, make sure the cake is level. You may have to slice off the top if it has become slightly domed during baking. However, it's not necessary to slice off the crust of each layer before frosting.

Slicing a Cake into Layers

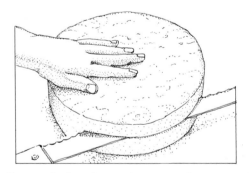

To slice a cake into layers, lay your palm on top of the cake and slowly turn the cake against the blade of a long serrated knife. Make a gentle sawing motion with the knife and rotate the cake until it is cut all the way around. Repeat the motion until the cake is sliced through. This is easiest done on a turntable. Slide an extra cardboard round or baking sheet underneath it.

Beveling

Beveling or rounding the upper edge of the cake gives it a smooth, custom shape that lends itself well to many of the cakes in this book. Beveling is done by slicing the top edge off the cake in a smooth and steady motion, moving in one complete circle at a time. The upper and lower edges are then trimmed for a smooth line. Beveling is easier on a well-chilled cake.

Beveling a Cake

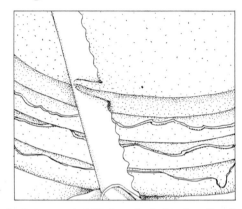

Fill the layers and chill the cake before beveling it. Hold a long serrated knife at a 45-degree angle and slice off the top rim of the cake so that it is slightly rounded. Trim the edges above and below this cut to smooth the angle. Do this with the cake on a turntable, if possible.

Changing a Cake's Shape

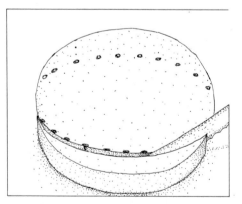

To cut a cake layer into another shape, hold a parchment paper template cut to the desired size on the cake. Mark the template edge with a toothpick and then remove the template. Using the marks left by the toothpick as a guide, cut the cake with a long serrated knife. Use the same template on all cake layers so that they will match when filled and stacked.

Squaring off a Cake

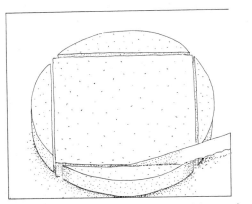

It's an easy matter to square off a round layer of cake. Lay it on a flat surface and mark off the square with toothpicks, using a ruler as a guide. Remove the toothpicks. Slice off the rounded edges with a long serrated knife.

Brushing a Cake with Liqueur or Syrup

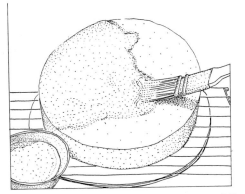

Brushing cake layers with a few tablespoons of liqueur or syrup—or a mixture of both—adds flavor and helps to keep the cake soft and moist. You may prefer to sprinkle the liquid on the cake by shaking the brush over the surface or dribbling it from a spoon.

Filling and Frosting the Cake

Cakes are filled to add richness and variety of texture and flavor. The flavor of the filling should complement that of the cake, not clash with it—bear this in mind if you are substituting different frostings and fillings from those specified. We give guidance on the amount of filling to use for each layer; if the filling is too generous, it will overwhelm the cake; if too meager, it may as well not be there at all.

Recipes for all the fillings and frosting are found in Chapter 2, with variations as well as storage tips.

Frosting a cake with buttercream, confectioners' sugar frosting, whipped cream, ganache, or fruit glazes does take a little time if you want a perfect, smooth finish without any crumbs peeking through to mar the effect.

Begin with a cool cake set on a cardboard round or platter or, ideally, on a turntable. Secure the cake to its base with a dot of icing. Invert one layer onto the plate or round, fill, and top with the second layer, upright. Frosting should be at room temperature before it is applied, with the exception of whipped cream, which is best kept chilled. If the cake has more than one layer, fill and stack the layers, and refrigerate the cake until the filling is firm—15 to 30 minutes.

Frosting a Cake

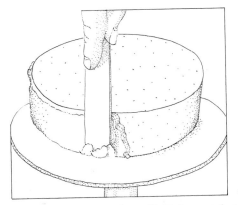

Frost the sides of the cake first. Hold the metal spatula with a dab of frosting against the cake, perpendicular to the turntable or platter. Move the spatula down and away from you without lifting it from the cake. Frost only a few inches of cake with each stroke.

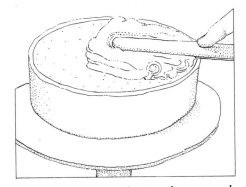

When the sides are covered, spread an even layer of frosting over the top of the cake. Refrigerate the frosted cake before applying a second layer of frosting.

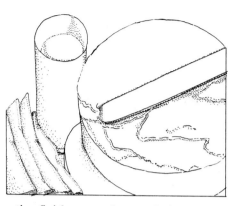

For a satiny finish, warm the spatula in hot water, wipe it dry, and use it to smooth the frosting.

When the filling has set, gently brush away loose crumbs and frost the sides. Scoop a generous dab of frosting onto the end of a metal spatula and hold it against the side of the cake, perpendicular to the turntable or platter. Without lifting the spatula from the cake, smooth the frosting around the sides of the cake, moving the spatula down and away from you. Scrape excess frosting and any crumbs from the spatula, and apply more frosting. Avoid getting any crumbs in the container of frosting. Don't expect to cover more than a few inches of cake with each application, and begin each stroke by overlapping the preceding bit just a little. When the sides are covered, spread an even layer of frosting over the top of the cake. This first coat of frosting seals the crumb and acts as the foundation for a smooth finish. Refrigerate the cake for 20 to 30 minutes to set the frosting. Repeat the procedure, beginning again with the sides and ending with the top. If you want an especially lush look, frost the cake a third time. But always wipe the spatula clean each time you lift it off the cake.

Frosting Dacquoise

Use the same frosting techniques for dacquoise, but first trim the layers so that they are of equal size. With a paring knife or scissors, cut away any irregularities in the dacquoise—remember to keep your touch light as dacquoise splinters easily. If it does break, put the broken layer in the center of the cake and cement it together as you spread the frosting. No matter how carefully you trim the dacquoise, you will probably have to build up the layers with some extra frosting to prevent a lopsided cake.

Marzipan

Marzipan, a sweetened almond paste, is available in seven-ounce packages, from bakers' supply houses, specialty stores and supermarkets. Roll it out as you would pie dough and drape it over a cake. With your fingers, gently pat and smooth the folds and creases on the sides; any tears can be patted together with your fingertips.

Refrigeration will cause marzipan to moisten. If you are fashioning marzipan shapes, they should be allowed to harden at room temperature for a few hours or longer before they are put on the cake.

Rolling Marzipan or Fondant

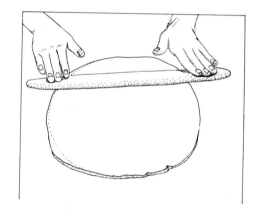

Working outward from the center, roll marzipan or rolled fondant out to a thickness of about 1/8 to 1/16 inch. A French rolling pin—one without handles—gives you more control.

Glazes

Shiny chocolate and fruit glazes—often apricot, raspberry, and currant—may act as an undercoat for other frosting or be used alone for a smooth finish and sheen. Either way, they help seal in a cake's moisture. To glaze a cake with either fruit or melted chocolate (or with poured fondant), first brush all the crumbs from the cake with your hand or a pastry brush. Put the cake on a cardboard round and then on a wire rack placed on a plate, baking sheet, or jelly roll pan to catch the excess glaze. Pour a generous amount of glaze, heated to tepid, over the center of the cake so that it flows over it and down the sides. You can encourage this with a spatula if necessary. Pick up any glaze that falls on the baking sheet with the spatula and reapply it to those parts of the cake that are not covered.

Pouring and Spreading Glaze

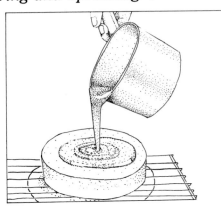

Put the cake on a cardboard round and then on a rack positioned over a plate, baking sheet, or jelly roll pan. Pour a generous amount of warmed glaze over the center of the cake.

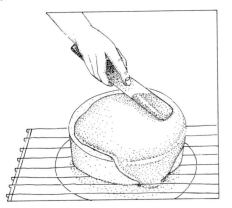

If it's necessary, coax the glaze evenly over the top and down the sides of the cake with a metal spatula. Scrape any excess glaze from the plate or pan. Strain and reapply it to the cake, if needed.

Using Food Colors

Frosting and decorations may be tinted to a rainbow of colors with liquid or paste food colorings. In most cases we recommend paste, as it offers a greater range of colors and will not alter the consistency of the frosting. Paste colors are easy to work with and can transform buttercream, royal icing, and marzipan into vibrant or subtle shades, as you wish.

Buttercream can be colored with liquid or paste colors. For the very palest of shades, use liquid. Royal icing nearly always requires paste colors; the oil present in many liquid colors will break down the icing and render it useless. Marzipan absorbs color very well; knead a little into the marzipan. As you knead, the color will intensify for the first two or three minutes. Add more color at this point for a darker shade. As the marzipan dries over several hours, the color will lighten. Pastillage has similar properties to marzipan and is best tinted with paste colors.

Experiment with color. We explain how to create colors in the frostings, marzipan, and pastillage in these recipes, but exercise your own color sense as well. A little brown color will transform an orangey shade of yellow and red into peach, but do add just a little. Create colors gradually, with tiny amounts of coloring; colors can be darkened but it is impossible to lighten a color that is too intense.

Decorating with a Pastry Bag

Piping decorations onto a cake is the most creative, imaginative aspect of home baking. Decorating with tips and learning to use a pastry bag generally requires a little patience and practice, but the results are terrifically rewarding.

Decorating tips come in a staggering range of shapes and sizes. The techniques shown in this book are done with small decorating tips, generally in plain, star, rose, leaf, petal, and basket weave patterns. The sizes and shapes are specified by number in each recipe.

Tips for Decorating

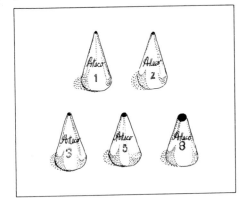

Round tips #1, 2, 3, 5, and 8.

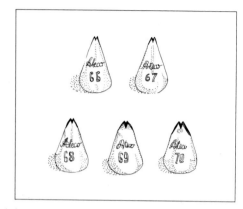

Leaf tips #66, 67, 68, 69, and 70.

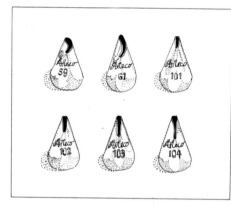

Rose tips #59, 61, 101, 102, 103, and 104.

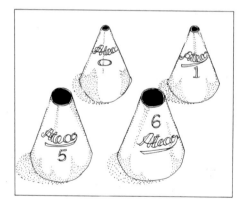

Large round tips #0, 1, 5, and 6.

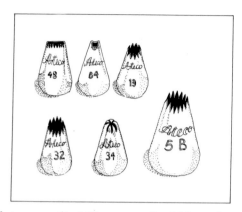

Basket weave tip #48, square tip #84, and star tips #19, 32, 34, and 5B.

When decorating with a pastry bag, fill it no more than about half or two-thirds full. This will give you more control over the pressure as you pipe. Fold down the end of the bag to form a cuff as you spoon in the frosting. Unfold the cuff and gently push the frosting down toward the tip. Squeeze a little frosting back into the bowl before you start to force out any air trapped inside, which would mar the piping.

Piping a Decorative Border

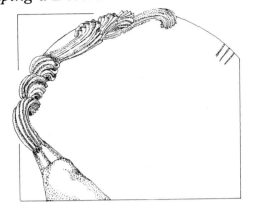

Bold swags and folds are accomplished by holding the bag at a low angle and exerting strong pressure. For a rhythmic border such as this one, make small marks on the cake to indicate where the pattern changes.

Making a Parchment Cone

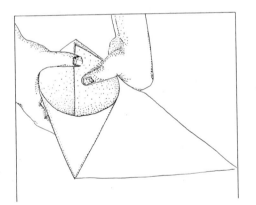

To make a parchment paper cone, cut a triangle with two equal sides, each 15 inches long, and a base of about 17 inches. Curl one of the base points over and position it on the apex (top point).

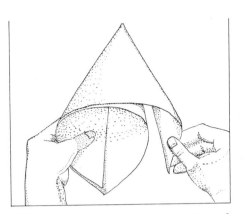

Wrap the remaining base point under the other two points. Pull the paper as you roll it so that it forms a tightly closed cone.

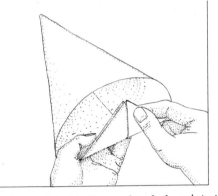

Fold all three points together and tuck them into the top of the cone to secure. With a pair of sharp scissors or a small knife, snip off the tip of the cone to the desired size. Parchment paper cones are most often used for delicate work requiring a very small opening.

Piping effects depend almost as much on the angle of the bag to the cake and the pressure applied as on the shape and size of the tip itself. For bold decorations like a thick star border or billowy folds of whipped cream, exert more pressure on the bag; delicate designs need only a light touch. A pastry bag is usually held at an angle of 45 to 90 degrees, depending on what shape you are piping. Exert steady pressure and move the bag smoothly and evenly.

For fine piping, work with only a small amount of frosting in the bag and a tiny tip. Exert minimum but steady pressure. You may find it easier to pipe fine lines, wisps, and swirls with a parchment paper cone. They are simple to make and the end can be snipped off to form a tiny opening.

If you're unsure of a piping technique or want to experiment, practice on a sheet of parchment or waxed paper, or on an inverted cake pan. Follow our instructions for decorating, or improvise your own designs. If you do make a mistake on the cake itself, first refrigerate it briefly and then you can try to gently scrape it off the cake with a toothpick or tip of a knife.

Piping Gel With a Parchment Cone

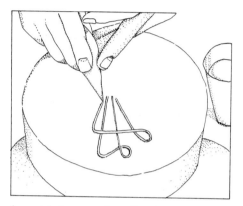

A parchment paper cone is well-suited for piping gel into fine lines and swirls. Hold the cone close to the surface of the cake at a high angle and exert steady, even pressure.

Storing Cakes

Filled but unfrosted cakes can be covered with plastic wrap and frozen for about two weeks without any loss of quality. Cakes frosted with buttercream can also be frozen. Freeze them unwrapped at first, to safeguard the frosting. When they are thoroughly frozen, wrap them loosely in plastic, but be sure they are completely sealed. Unwrap the cake and defrost it either at room temperature or in the refrigerator for slow, steady defrosting.

Generally, cakes frosted with buttercream, confectioners' sugar, or ganache may be stored in the refrigerator for two to three days or at cool room temperature for a day. Cover them loosely with plastic, tucking it under the plate or cardboard round to seal the cake so it doesn't pick up any refrigerator odor. If you are not serving the cake immediately, it's best just to keep it in a cool, safe place.

Cakes decorated with marzipan or rolled fondant should not be refrigerated, as the humidity will cause the marzipan or fondant to loosen. A coating of marzipan or fondant keeps the cake fresh, so refrigeration isn't necessary in any case. A cake frosted with buttercream and decorated with marzipan or rolled fondant shapes may be refrigerated in the normal way.

Buttercream flowers formed on flower nails may be frozen on their waxed paper squares for up to a week. Allow them to harden unwrapped in the freezer and then wrap them well with foil or plastic wrap. Position the frozen flowers on the cake while they are firm, and allow the cake to come to room temperature before serving.

Transporting Cakes

Cakes are most easily carried in cardboard cake boxes, which are available from bakers' supply stores. Place the cake on a cardboard base slightly larger than the cake before slipping it into the box to ensure that the sides of the box do not touch the cake. Bring along a little extra frosting, a pastry bag, and appropriate tips to make last-minute repairs at your destination.

Serving

Cakes should be brought to room temperature before serving; generally a half-hour out of the refrigerator is enough. Cut the cake with a serrated knife—wiping it clean after each cut—and save the cake spatula for lifting each slice to the serving plate.

As a final caveat, we recommend several important steps before beginning any cake. The recipe should be read through from beginning to end. Although this point may seem obvious, it cannot be overly emphasized.

Enough time should be allowed to thoroughly mix, bake, assemble, and decorate the cake. Additionally, chilling time should also be considered, as indicated in each recipe.

All the ingredients must be assembled beforehand. A missing ingredient, however small in quantity, can doom a cake. The ingredients should be assembled at room temperature, unless otherwise specified. Remember that butter and flour for prepared pans are not included in the ingredients, so be sure to have enough on hand. Utensils and other equipment, too, must be organized before baking begins. Finally, allow your oven to preheat well in advance of the time the cake will be baked.

Keeping these tips in mind and using the basic recipes and the techniques we've outlined, even an inexperienced baker will be able to come up with his or her own satisfying creations.

CHAPTER TWO

Recipes

The recipes in this chapter are the building blocks of our decorated cakes. Besides recipes for basic genoise, layer cake, pound cake, dacquoise, nut cake, and fruitcake, variations allow you to make a lemon cake, chocolate cake, spice, or orange cake. Each may be filled or frosted with one of the buttercreams, confectioners' sugar frostings, ganaches, pastry cream, or fruit glazes. If you want to add crunch to a filling with a handful of chopped praline or shape a fantastic flower of pastillage, these recipes will prove infinitely adaptable.

Throughout the book we make suggestions for the type of cake to bake before you even begin to think about decorating. In making these recommendations we have considered the balance between the taste and texture of the cake and the frosting and filling. For example, we rarely spread sweet, rich buttercream on a layer cake. These cakes, sometimes called butter cakes, are so rich themselves that the addition of buttercream could be construed as overkill. Still, use your own recipes if you prefer, and if time is a factor, use a mix. If you'd like to create a pure white cake with a mocha mousse filling, don't hesitate to make one simply because we have not—but do keep the size and proportions of the decorations in mind when designing a cake.

When you are choosing a frosting or glaze, we urge a little more caution. Not all frostings stand up to the same decorating procedures. This is particularly true with decorations that are piped through a pastry bag. For the most part, we've used buttercream for piping. Our recipe is a tried-and-true one, and unless you have one of your own that you are very comfortable with, we suggest you use ours. This applies for royal icing, pastillage, and rolled fondant.

Genoise

Anyone who has enjoyed cakes from a French bakery or patisserie will probably recognize genoise by its delicate, light spongecake texture and delicious buttery flavor. For sheer versatility, no other cake compares with genoise. This wonderful cake works beautifully with rich buttercream, fresh fruit and whipped cream, dark chocolate ganache, even with just a dusting of confectioners' sugar. Genoise batter can be flavored with chocolate, coffee, fruit, or for a slightly heavier cake, with ground nuts. A sprinkling of liqueur such as Cointreau or Grand Marnier will help to retain its moistness.

Genoise is made without a leavening ingredient such as baking powder. Instead, its lightness is a result of carefully beating the eggs to a high volume. When baked, the air trapped by the eggs causes the batter to rise. We recommend warming the eggs over simmering water before beating to help expand them, but be careful not to heat them beyond the lukewarm stage. Take care also not to overbeat the batter, as this will result in a coarse, uneven texture and the cake will rise too high during baking, and then fall.

Though the mixing techniques demanded by genoise may seem complicated, once you have mastered them they will reward you with light, beautifully golden, and absolutely delicious cake layers.

Makes two 8-inch round layers or one 11½- by 15½-inch sheet cake
Serves 8 to 10
Preparation time 25 to 30 minutes
Baking time 15 to 30 minutes

6 eggs, at room temperature

1 cup sugar

1 cup flour, sifted with a pinch of salt

1 teaspoon vanilla extract

3 tablespoons sweet butter, melted

1. Preheat the oven to 350°. Set a pan one third full of water on to simmer. Lightly butter and flour two 8-inch round pans or one 11½- by 15½-inch jelly roll pan.

2. In the bowl of an electric mixer, lightly whisk together the eggs and sugar. Place the bowl over the simmering water—the bowl should not touch the water or the eggs will cook rather than heat—and continue whisking until the mixture is lukewarm and the sugar has almost dissolved, 3 to 4 minutes. Test with your finger to gauge the warmth of the eggs.

3. When the mixture is lukewarm, beat with an electric mixer at high speed just until it becomes pale and thick—2 to 3 minutes. The mixture has

been sufficiently beaten when it falls in a thick ribbon from a rubber spatula and sits on top of the batter for several seconds before sinking.

4. Remove the bowl from the mixer. Using a rubber spatula, gently sift the sifted flour into the batter one-third at a time. Fold only until the flour is incorporated. Add the vanilla and the melted butter, folding only until the liquid is distributed throughout the batter.

5. Pour the batter into the prepared pan(s) and bake in the center of the oven for 20 to 30 minutes for round pans or 15 to 20 minutes for a jelly roll pan. The cake is done when it pulls away slightly from the sides of the pan, springs back lightly when touched, and when a skewer or toothpick inserted into the center comes out clean.

6. Cool the cake(s) in the pan(s) on wire racks. Remove from the pan(s) while still slightly warm and allow to cool completely on the racks.

Chocolate Genoise

⅓ cup unsweetened cocoa

Reduce the flour to ⅔ cup. Sift the flour, cocoa, and salt together three times. Fold into the beaten egg and sugar mixture as directed.

Coconut Genoise

¼ cup unsweetened grated coconut

Reduce the flour to ¾ cup. Fold in the coconut after the flour has been incorporated into the batter.

Coffee Genoise

1 tablespoon instant coffee

1 tablespoon hot water

Dissolve the instant coffee in the hot water, and allow to cool. Add this mixture to the batter with the vanilla and melted butter.

Lemon Genoise

Grated zest and juice of 2 lemons

Add the juice and grated zest to the melted butter. Omit the vanilla extract.

Nut Genoise

½ cup ground nuts: almonds; toasted, skinned hazelnuts; walnuts; pecans; or Brazil nuts

Reduce the flour to ¾ cup. Add the ground nuts to the batter alternately with the sifted flour. The texture of the cake will depend on how finely the nuts have been ground. If they are rather coarse, toss them with a little flour so they do not sink to the bottom of the cake during baking.

Orange Genoise

Grated zest of ½ orange

Add the grated zest to the melted butter. You may also add the juice of ½ lemon, to enhance the citrus flavor.

Poppy Seed Genoise

2 tablespoons poppy seeds

1 teaspoon almond extract

Fold the poppy seeds into the batter after adding the flour, and substitute the almond extract for the vanilla.

■

Yellow Layer Cake

Often the first cake many of us ever taste, yellow layer cakes have been the proud issue of American kitchens for generations. The cake's rich color and fine crumb are as familiar as the glossy chocolate frosting that often graced it.

Makes two 8-inch round layers
Serves 8 to 10
Preparation time 15 to 20 minutes
Baking time 25 to 30 minutes

2 cups cake flour

3 teaspoons baking powder

¼ teaspoon salt

¾ cup sweet butter, at room temperature

1½ cups sugar

3 eggs, at room temperature

1 teaspoon vanilla extract, or the seeds from ½ vanilla bean

¾ cup milk, at room temperature

1. Preheat the oven to 350°. Butter and flour two 8-inch round pans.

2. Sift together the flour, baking powder, and salt. Set aside.

3. With an electric mixer at high speed, cream the butter until pale and smooth—1 to 2 minutes. Add the sugar gradually, mixing at medium speed until the mixture is light and fluffy. Add the eggs one at a time and continue to beat until the mixture lightens—about 2 minutes. Scrape the bottom and sides of the bowl often with a rubber spatula.

4. Add the vanilla extract or seeds to the milk. To add seeds, slit the bean lengthwise with a sharp knife and scrape them from the pod.

5. Fold the sifted dry ingredients into the mixture one-third at a time, alternating with the milk. Begin and end with the dry ingredients.

6. Divide the mixture between the prepared pans and bake for 25 to 30 minutes, until a toothpick inserted in the center comes out clean.

7. Cool the layers in the pans on wire racks. Remove them from the pans while still slightly warm, and allow to cool completely on the racks.

Almond Orange Cake

Zest and juice of 1 orange

⅔ cup almonds

Cut the zest from the skin of the orange with a sharp paring knife. Trim off the bitter white pith. In a food processor fitted with a metal blade, grind the zest with the almonds. Add this mixture to the batter with the dry ingredients.

Lemon Cake

¼ cup lemon juice

2 tablespoons grated lemon zest

Combine the lemon juice and grated zest (you will need about 2 lemons) and add to the batter as the last step. Omit the vanilla extract.

Orange Cake

Grated zest and juice of 1 orange

Combine the juice and grated zest and mix into the batter as the last step. (Do not omit the vanilla extract.)

■

Chocolate Layer Cake

Real chocolate infuses this luscious cake with the intense flavor often missing from those made from cocoa.

Makes two 8-inch round layers
Serves 8 to 10
Preparation time 25 to 30 minutes
Baking time 25 to 30 minutes

1 tablespoon lemon juice or vinegar

¾ cup milk, at room temperature

2 teaspoons vanilla extract

3 ounces unsweetened chocolate, coarsely chopped

¾ cup boiling water

¾ cup sweet butter, at room temperature

2 cups sugar

3 eggs, at room temperature

2¼ cups flour

1½ teaspoons baking soda

½ teaspoon salt

¾ teaspoon baking powder

1. Preheat the oven to 350°. Butter and flour two 8-inch round pans.

2. Add the lemon juice or vinegar to the milk to sour it. (You may substitute ¾ cup buttermilk for the sour milk, if desired.) Add the vanilla extract.

3. Place the chocolate in a bowl and pour the boiling water over it. Stir until the chocolate has melted and allow to cool.

4. In an electric mixer at high speed, cream the butter until pale and smooth—1 to 2 minutes. Gradually add the sugar, beating at medium speed until the mixture is light and fluffy. Add the eggs one at a time, blending thoroughly and scraping the sides and bottom of the bowl after each addition with a rubber spatula. Add the melted chocolate and mix just until blended.

5. Sift together the flour, baking soda, salt, and baking powder. With the mixer on low speed, add the sifted dry ingredients to the butter mixture a third at a time, alternating with the milk. Begin and end with the dry ingredients. Scrape the bottom and sides of the bowl frequently and mix only until blended after each addition.

6. Pour the mixture into the prepared pans and bake for 20 to 25 minutes, until a toothpick inserted in the center comes out clean.

7. Cool the layers in their pans on wire racks. Remove from pans while still slightly warm and allow to cool completely on the racks.

■

Pound Cake

Favored for its velvety texture and mellow flavor, pound cake can be dressed up with anything from poached fruit to chocolate sauce or enjoyed by itself. The cake keeps well, remaining moist and rich after a day or two.

Makes one 6-inch round cake or one 9- by 5-inch loaf
Serves 8 to 10
Preparation time 15 to 20 minutes
Baking time 45 to 55 minutes

2 cups flour

1½ teaspoons baking soda

Pinch of salt

Grated zest and juice of 1 lemon

1 teaspoon vanilla extract

2 tablespoons sour cream

1 cup sweet butter, at room temperature

1 cup sugar

5 eggs, separated, at room temperature

1. Preheat the oven to 350°. Lightly butter and flour the pan.

2. Sift together the flour, baking soda, and salt.

3. In a small bowl, mix together the lemon juice, grated lemon zest, vanilla extract, and sour cream.

4. With an electric mixer at high speed, cream the butter with half the sugar until light and fluffy—1 to 2 minutes.

5. Add the egg yolks and beat until the mixture is smooth and light-colored—about 2 minutes.

6. Using a rubber spatula, gradually fold the sifted flour into the mixture, alternating with the flavored sour cream. Scrape the sides and bottom

of the bowl occasionally while mixing. Fold only until the flour is thoroughly incorporated.

7. In a large bowl, whip the egg whites at medium speed until they form soft peaks. Increase to high speed and gradually add the remaining ½ cup of sugar. Stir a quarter of the egg whites into the batter to lighten it, then fold in the remaining whites. The batter will be stiff, even after adding the whites.

8. Scrape the batter into the pan and bake at 350° for 40 minutes for the round cake and about 55 minutes for the loaf. Cool the cake, still in the pan, on a wire rack and remove it from the pan while still slightly warm.

■

Spice Cake

Coriander gives this cake its distinctive, sharp flavor—the perfect complement to sweet frostings.

Makes two 8-inch round layers
Serves 8 to 10
Preparation time 15 to 20 minutes
Baking time 25 to 30 minutes

1 tablespoon lemon juice or vinegar

1 cup milk, at room temperature

½ teaspoon vanilla extract

½ teaspoon orange extract (optional)

½ cup sweet butter, at room temperature

1 cup sugar

3 eggs, at room temperature

2¼ cups flour

1 tablespoon ground coriander

1 teaspoon ground cinnamon

1 teaspoon ground nutmeg

¼ teaspoon ground cloves

1½ teaspoons baking powder

1½ teaspoons baking soda

¼ teaspoon salt

1. Preheat the oven to 350°. Butter and flour two 8-inch round pans.

2. Add the lemon juice or vinegar to the milk to sour it (you may substitute one cup buttermilk for the sour milk, if desired). Stir in the vanilla and orange extracts.

3. With an electric mixer at high speed, cream the butter until pale and smooth—1 to 2 minutes. Add the sugar, mixing at medium speed until the mixture is light and fluffy.

4. Add the eggs one at a time, scraping the sides and bottom of the bowl often with a rubber spatula and mixing well after each addition.

5. Sift together the flour, spices, baking powder, baking soda, and salt. Add one third of the sifted dry ingredients to the batter and mix well. Add a third of the milk, mix, and continue adding the remaining dry ingredients a third at a time, alternating with the milk. Scrape the sides and bottom of the bowl well, and mix only until the ingredients are thoroughly combined.

6. Pour the batter into the prepared pans. Bake in the preheated oven for 25 to 30 minutes, until a toothpick inserted in the center comes out clean.

7. Cool the layers in the pans on wire racks. Remove them from pans while still slightly warm and allow to cool completely on the racks.

■

Nut Cake

Denser than a nut génoise, with a rich nutty flavor, this cake will take on the character of whichever nut is used.

Makes two 8-inch round layers
Serves 8 to 10
Preparation time 20 to 25 minutes
Baking time 25 to 30 minutes

¾ cup sweet butter, at room temperature

⅔ cup brown sugar

3 eggs, separated, at room temperature

2 cups flour

1½ teaspoons baking soda

¼ teaspoon salt

1 cup crushed, chopped, or ground walnuts, pecans, toasted skinned hazelnuts, or Brazil nuts

1 teaspoon vanilla extract

1 cup sour cream, at room temperature

¼ cup granulated sugar

1. Preheat the oven to 350°. Lightly butter and flour two 8-inch round pans.

2. With an electric mixer at high speed, cream the butter until pale and smooth. Gradually add the brown sugar, beating at medium speed until the mixture is light and fluffy. Add the egg yolks one at a time, and continue to beat until the mixture lightens further—1 to 2 minutes. Stop the machine and scrape the bottom and sides of the bowl occasionally with a rubber spatula.

3. Sift together the flour, baking soda, and salt. Toss ½ cup of this mixture with the nuts to coat them so they will be evenly distributed throughout the layers.

4. Stir the vanilla extract into the sour cream.

5. Gradually add the sifted dry ingredients to the butter mixture, alternating with the coated nuts and the sour cream.

6. In a clean bowl, beat the egg whites at medium speed until they form soft peaks. Increase the speed to high and gradually add the granulated sugar. Continue beating until the whites form stiff peaks.

7. Stir about a third of the egg whites into the batter to lighten it. Fold in the remaining whites.

8. Pour the batter into the prepared pans. Bake in the preheated oven for 25 to 30 minutes, until a toothpick inserted in the center comes out clean.

9. Cool the layers in the pans on wire racks. Remove them from pans while still slightly warm, and allow to cool completely on the racks.

Pistachio Nut Cake

Use 1 cup chopped or ground unsalted pistachios, and substitute granulated sugar for the brown sugar and almond extract for the vanilla.

■

Fruitcake

Generously studded with dried fruit and nuts and livened with spices, this fruitcake is delicious just after baking and it will age gracefully. To store the cake, wrap it in cheesecloth dampened with brandy, then wrap well in foil. Remoisten the cheesecloth once a week.

Makes one 6-inch round cake or 9- by 5-inch loaf
Serves 8 to 10
Preparation time 35 to 40 minutes
Baking time 55 minutes

1 cup sweet butter, at room temperature

⅓ cup sugar

2 eggs, at room temperature

½ teaspoon cinnamon

¼ teaspoon allspice

¼ teaspoon ground cloves

¼ teaspoon mace

¼ teaspoon baking soda

¼ teaspoon salt

1 cup flour

½ cup dark raisins

½ cup white raisins

1 cup currants

6 dried figs, chopped

4 dates, chopped

5 dried apricot halves, chopped

¼ cup dried apple slices, chopped

1 tablespoon candied ginger, chopped

1 tablespoon diced citron

1 cup pecan pieces

3 tablespoons plus ¼ cup brandy

1. Preheat the oven to 325°. Line the bottom of the pan with brown or parchment paper and butter both the paper and the sides of the pan.

2. With an electric mixer at high speed, cream the butter until pale and smooth—1 to 2 minutes. Add the sugar gradually, beating at medium speed until the mixture is light and fluffy. Add the eggs one at a time, scraping the sides and bottom of the bowl several times with a rubber spatula.

3. Sift the spices, the baking soda, and the salt with 1 cup minus 2 tablespoons of flour.

4. Toss the dried fruit and nuts in the remaining 2 tablespoons of flour to prevent them from sticking together.

5. Add 3 tablespoons of brandy to the butter mixture and mix well. Gradually add the sifted flour and spices, mixing well. Fold in the dried fruit and nuts.

6. Place a shallow baking pan filled with hot water on the floor of the preheated oven—this steams the fruitcake and keeps it from drying out. Pour the mixture into the prepared pan and bake for about 55 minutes.

7. The cake is done when a skewer inserted in the center comes out clean and the cake springs back slightly when touched. Remove the cake from the oven and, while still hot, pour the remaining ¼ cup of brandy over it. Cool the cake on a wire rack before removing it from the pan.

■

Dense Chocolate Cake

Try this cake on any confirmed chocolate lover—it is always a success. During baking, the cake may crack on the top and after baking it may fall, but neither affects the texture or flavor.

Makes one 8-inch round layer
Serves 6 to 8
Preparation time 15 to 20 minutes
Baking time 40 minutes

8 ounces semisweet chocolate

1 cup sweet butter

¼ cup heavy cream, at room temperature

5 eggs, separated

¼ cup sugar

½ cup fresh breadcrumbs

½ cup flour

1. Preheat the oven to 325°. Lightly butter and flour an 8-inch pan, preferably a springform.

2. Place the chocolate and the butter in a bowl set over a pan of hot but not simmering water and stir until melted. Stir in the cream.

3. In an electric mixer at medium speed, beat the egg yolks with the sugar until thick and light— about 2 minutes. Add the chocolate mixture and stir to blend. Fold in the breadcrumbs and flour.

4. In a separate bowl, whisk the egg whites until stiff peaks form. Stir about a quarter of the whites into the batter to lighten it, then fold in the remainder, about a third at a time. Pour the mixture into the prepared pan.

5. Bake for about 40 minutes, until the cake tests clean about 2 inches from the side. This cake should not test clean at the center, which remains intentionally moist.

6. Cool the cake in its pan on a wire rack. Remove the springform sides while the cake is slightly

warm and invert onto a wire rack, or allow to cool on the metal base. Chill the cake before decorating.

■

Dacquoise

Although almost as light as air, dacquoise is surprisingly flavorful: Its crisp, chewy layers will melt in your mouth. Like meringue, dacquoise is made with egg whites whipped to stiff peaks and sweetened with sugar and vanilla, but is also flavored with ground hazelnuts or almonds. The nuts give dacquoise an intriguing texture and cut the cloying sweetness often associated with meringue. Dacquoise batter is spooned into a pastry bag and piped into layers on a baking sheet. As it bakes, dacquoise will expand slightly and retain the shape it was piped to, becoming crispy and brittle. When cool, the layers are treated as cake, filled and frosted with buttercream or ganache, sometimes sandwiched between layers of genoise.

Makes three 8-inch layers
Serves 8 to 10
Preparation time 25 minutes
Baking time 35 minutes

3 egg whites, at room temperature

⅛ teaspoon cream of tartar

½ teaspoon vanilla extract

¾ cup sugar

¼ cup ground almonds or toasted skinned hazelnuts

2 tablespoons cornstarch

1. Preheat the oven to 300°. Using a cake pan or pie plate, trace three 8-inch circles on paper. Turn paper upside down to line baking sheets.

2. In an electric mixer, beat the egg whites and cream of tartar at medium speed until soft peaks form. Turn to high speed and add the vanilla and ½ cup of the sugar a tablespoon at a time, beating until the meringue forms stiff peaks.

3. Mix the remaining ¼ cup of sugar with the ground nuts and cornstarch. Sprinkle a third of this mixture onto the meringue and with a rubber spatula fold in gently but quickly (the meringue will fall as you fold). Fold in the remaining sugar mixture a third at a time.

4. Spoon the batter into a pastry bag fitted with an Ateco #5 large tip (or a plain tip no bigger than ½-inch diameter). Pipe the batter in concentric circles, working from the center outward, until the layer is 8 inches in diameter. Repeat for the second and third layers.

5. Bake in the preheated oven for 35 minutes, until the layers are dry and brittle to the touch. Turn the oven off and allow the dacquoise to cool to room temperature in the oven—about 1 hour.

Chocolate Dacquoise

3 egg whites, at room temperature

⅛ teaspoon cream of tartar

½ teaspoon vanilla or almond extract

¾ cup sugar

2 tablespoons unsweetened cocoa

1 tablespoon cornstarch

2 tablespoons ground almonds or toasted skinned hazelnuts

Preheat the oven to 300°. Proceed as for dacquoise, following Steps 1 and 2. Sift the remaining ¼ cup sugar with the cocoa and cornstarch. Stir the ground nuts into the sugar and cocoa mixture. Fold into the beaten egg whites a third at a time. Continue as for dacquoise.

■

Swiss Meringue Buttercream

Smooth, heavenly buttercream can be lavished on any number of cakes, and this basic recipe for Swiss Meringue Buttercream can be flavored in dozens of ways. Sometimes as fillings but more often as frostings and decoration, buttercreams are used on many of the cakes in this book. It is more temperamental than shortening-based frostings but there is simply no comparison in flavor and texture.

To begin buttercream, egg whites and sugar are whisked together while being gently warmed over simmering water. The whites are then beaten to a stiff meringue and sweet butter is added a tablespoon at a time.

Having the meringue and butter at the right temperature during mixing is one key to successful buttercream. Before adding the butter, the meringue should be at room temperature—spoon out a dollop from the center of the bowl and test with your finger. If you add the butter before the mixture is cool, it will melt and the buttercream will be runny. The butter should be cold yet malleable—not hard. If it is too cold, the buttercream will be difficult to mix and will contain tiny pieces of unblended butter. If it is too soft, the buttercream will be too loose to spread.

Sometimes the buttercream "breaks" just after the butter has been added. If this happens, continue to beat just until smooth again, no longer.

Excessive beating, caused by adding the butter too slowly, may also make the buttercream too loose. If this happens, refrigerate the buttercream for 10 to 15 minutes and rebeat.

This recipe generously fills and frosts two 8- or 10-inch layers. Leftover buttercream can be refrigerated in an airtight container for up to 2 weeks.

Makes about 4 cups
Preparation time 35 to 40 minutes

½ cup egg whites (from 3 to 4 eggs)

1 cup sugar

1¼ cups sweet butter, cold but not hard

1. Cut the butter into tablespoon-size pieces. Place the egg whites and sugar in the bowl of an electric mixer over a pan one-third full of simmering water (the bowl should not touch the water or the mixture will cook rather than heat). Whisk until the sugar is partially dissolved and the mixture is warm.

2. Using an electric mixer, whip the mixture at high speed until it forms stiff peaks. Reduce the speed to medium and continue beating until the meringue cools to room temperature.

3. Beating at medium speed, add the butter one piece at a time. Stop the machine occasionally to scrape the sides and bottom of the bowl with a rubber spatula. When all the butter has been added, increase to high speed and beat just until the buttercream is smooth and light.

4. Any flavoring should be added at this point. Add liquids slowly, with the mixer at medium speed. Add dry flavorings all at once. After the flavoring has been added, scrape the bottom and sides of the bowl and the beaters, and beat briefly at high speed.

Amaretto

Add ¼ cup Amaretto liqueur and 1 tablespoon vanilla extract.

Cassis

Add ½ cup currant jelly and 2 tablespoons Creme de Cassis.

Chestnut

Add 8 ounces sweetened chestnut puree.

Chocolate

Add 8 ounces semisweet chocolate, melted and slightly cooled.

Coconut

Add ¼ cup cream of coconut.

Coffee

Add 3 tablespoons instant espresso or other coffee, dissolved in 1 tablespoon of hot water.

Lemon

Add finely grated zest and juice of 3 lemons.

Orange

Add juice of 1 orange and finely grated zest of 2 oranges.

Praline

Add ¾ cup ground praline.

White Chocolate

Add 8 ounces white chocolate, melted and slightly cooled.

Liqueur-flavored Buttercream

You can also flavor buttercream with spirits such as cognac, rum, kirsch, framboise, and Grand Marnier. Add 3 to 4 tablespoons, according to taste.

■

Confectioners' Sugar Frosting

Makes 3 cups
Preparation time 8 to 10 minutes

¾ cup sweet butter, at room temperature

4 cups confectioners' sugar

6 tablespoons heavy cream

1 tablespoon vanilla extract

1. With an electric mixer at high speed, cream the butter until pale and fluffy. Reduce the speed and add the confectioners' sugar a cup at a time. Mix the frosting until blended, scraping the sides and bottom of the bowl frequently with a rubber spatula.

2. Gradually add the cream and the vanilla extract. Increase the speed and beat until the frosting is light and spreadable.

Chocolate Frosting

Add 4 ounces melted, cooled unsweetened chocolate with the cream.

■

Whipped Cream

Two cups heavy cream will yield about four cups of whipped cream, enough to fill and frost a three-layer 8-inch cake generously.

In especially hot, humid weather, chill the bowl and beaters before whipping the cold cream. If you can, use heavy cream rather than whipping cream as it has a slightly higher butterfat content and will whip to a stiffer consistency.

Whip the cream only until it forms stiff peaks. Over-whipping causes the butterfat to coagulate and gives the cream a granular look.

2 cups heavy cream

Beat the cream in the bowl of an electric mixer at medium speed. As the cream begins to reach the soft peak stage, watch it closely to prevent overbeating. When it thickens, remove the bowl from the mixer and whisk the cream by hand until it forms stiff peaks.

Sweetened Whipped Cream

Whipped cream may be sweetened to taste—1 tablespoon of sugar to 2 cups of cream is the usual amount, but more sugar may be added if desired. When sweetening cream, a tablespoon of vanilla extract will enhance the flavor.

Cream may be sweetened with confectioners', superfine, or granulated sugar.

Chocolate Whipped Cream

Makes 2 cups

1 cup heavy cream

3 ounces semisweet chocolate, melted and cooled.

Whip the cream to soft peaks. Fold one-third of the whipped cream into the cooled chocolate. When it has been incorporated, fold in the balance of the cream. Whip the cream to stiff peaks stage.

■

Ganache

Ganache is a devastatingly delicious combination of chocolate and heavy cream. When warm, ganache is thin enough to pour over a cake and will remain dark and shiny. You may cool ganache to room temperature, which will thicken it slightly, and beat it with an electric beater to a lighter color and thicker consistency. In this case, use it immediately or the ganache will become solid and impossible to spread. However, it may be beaten again to soften it, if necessary.

Makes 2½ cups
Preparation time 8 to 10 minutes

1 pound semisweet chocolate

1 cup heavy cream

1. Chop the chocolate into matchstick-size pieces and place in a mixing bowl.

2. Bring the cream to a boil and immediately pour onto the chopped chocolate. Stir until smooth and then strain through a medium sieve.

3. Ganache may be flavored with ground nuts or liqueurs. Use 2 tablespoons to ¼ cup of nuts or liqueur, according to taste. Add these flavorings at the end.

Ganache Glaze

This variation of ganache is poured over a cake as a glaze. As the ganache cools, it will thicken and become stiff. If you need to thin it, set it over a pan half-full of barely simmering water, being careful not to overheat—the bottom of the bowl should not touch the water; the bowl shouldn't be so hot that you cannot touch it to pick it up; and the water in the pan should never boil, just barely simmer.

Makes 3 cups
Preparation time 8 to 10 minutes

1 pound semisweet chocolate

1½ cups heavy cream

1. Make the ganache following the directions above. The extra cream will give it a pouring consistency.

2. Set the cake on a wire rack placed on a baking sheet to catch excess glaze. Pour the glaze over the cake. The excess glaze may be strained and used again.

Butter Ganache

As its name suggests, this is a richer, buttery version of ganache; the butter makes it very easy to spread.

Makes 3½ cups
Preparation time 15 minutes

1 pound semisweet chocolate

1½ cups heavy cream

6 tablespoons sweet butter, cold

1. Make the ganache following the directions above.

2. When the mixture is smooth, stir in the butter 1 tablespoon at a time, waiting until each piece has melted before adding the next. This will produce a shiny, dark mixture that spreads easily.

■

Royal Icing

Crisp and brilliant white, this is the frosting often used for the most delicate piping.

The recipe yields more than you will probably need for any one cake. To keep the icing from hardening, cover with plastic wrap and place a damp towel over the top. If the towel is kept damp, the icing will keep for 3 to 4 weeks in the refrigerator. Stored icing must be rebeaten before using.

Makes 1¼ cups
Preparation time 10 to 12 minutes

1 egg white

⅛ teaspoon cream of tartar

1¼ to 1½ cups confectioners' sugar

1. Place the egg white and the cream of tartar in a large stainless steel or non-aluminum bowl.

2. Add 1¼ cups of sugar and beat with an electric mixer until blended. The mixture should fall heavily from a spoon without sticking: if it pours, it is too thin and will need some or all of

the remaining ¼ cup of sugar to achieve the right consistency.

3. Continue to beat for 3 to 4 minutes, until the mixture is thick and white and has a creamy consistency.

4. When using the icing, cover the portion still in the bowl with a damp towel, making sure that the towel does not touch the icing. This will keep it from hardening.

■

Pastry Cream

Most recognizable perhaps as the filling in eclairs and napoleons, pastry cream is a light custard of eggs, sugar, cream, and butter. We have used this cream as a filling in several cakes as a smooth contrast to cake, marzipan, or ganache.

Makes 2 cups
Preparation time 10 to 12 minutes

1 egg

2 egg yolks

2 tablespoons cornstarch

2 tablespoons flour

⅓ cup plus 2 tablespoons sugar

1½ cups milk

½ cup heavy cream

½ teaspoon vanilla extract

½ tablespoon sweet butter

1. With a wire whisk, beat the egg and yolks together in a bowl. Sift the cornstarch, the flour, and ⅓ cup of sugar into the beaten eggs. Whisk the mixture until smooth.

2. In a 1-quart, heavy bottom saucepan, combine the milk and cream with the 2 tablespoons of sugar and bring to a rising boil. Remove from the heat. Whisk half the hot milk into the egg mixture. Then pour the milk-and-egg mixture back

into the saucepan with the remaining hot milk. Stir over low heat until the mixture is just coming to a boil, with large bubbles forming and bursting at the sides of the pan. Be sure to stir constantly and get into the angles of the pan, to prevent lumps forming.

3. Stir in the vanilla and the butter. Strain the mixture through a medium sieve into a bowl and cover with plastic wrap. Make sure the wrap touches the surface, as this prevents skin from forming. The cream may be refrigerated for up to 4 days, but should not be frozen.

Variations

Omit the vanilla and add flavorings last, when you are stirring in the butter.

Chocolate

Add 3 ounces semisweet chocolate, melted.

Coffee

Add 1½ tablespoons instant coffee dissolved in 1 tablespoon hot water.

Lemon

Add grated zest and juice of 2 lemons.

Liqueurs

Add 2 tablespoons, or to taste.

Orange

Add grated zest and juice of 1 orange.

■

Almond Cream

Almond cream is almond paste blended with cream. We find it is a wonderful filling in grand wedding cakes, with its characteristic almond flavor and creamy texture.

Makes 1¾ cups
Preparation time 15 to 20 minutes

3½ ounces almond paste

1 cup heavy cream

1. Place the almond paste in the large bowl of an electric mixer fitted with a paddle attachment. With the mixer at low speed, slowly add ¼ cup of the cream and beat to loosen the paste. Gradually increasing the speed, beat until the mixture is light and fluffy.

2. Change to the whip attachment. Add the remaining cream and beat until the mixture is spreadable, increasing the speed from medium to high—5 to 10 minutes. Do not overwhip or the cream will curdle.

∎

Crème Anglaise

Not as thick as pastry cream, crème anglaise is sweet sauce.

Makes 2½ cups
Preparation time 10 minutes

4 egg yolks

3 tablespoons sugar

2 cups half-and-half

½ vanilla bean

1. Whisk together the yolks and 2 tablespoons of the sugar until smooth.

2. Scald the half-and-half with the remaining tablespoon of sugar and the vanilla bean.

3. Stir a third of the scalded cream into the yolk mixture and return it to the pan. Stir over low heat, using a wooden spoon, until the mixture is slightly thickened and coats the back of a metal spoon. Do not let the custard boil.

4. Strain the crème anglaise through a fine sieve into a bowl, remove the vanilla bean, and allow to cool. Refrigerate in an airtight container.

∎

Chocolate Mousse

One of our favorite pairings is any delicate cake and this light, heady chocolate mousse.

Makes 2½ cups
Preparation time 30 to 40 minutes

9 ounces semisweet chocolate

¾ cup sweet butter, at room temperature

4 eggs, separated, at room temperature

2 tablespoons rum, bourbon, or liqueur

¼ cup sugar

¾ cup heavy cream

1. Coarsely chop the chocolate. Put the chocolate and the butter in a bowl and melt over a pan of barely simmering water, stirring frequently. Remove from heat and cool slightly.

2. Whisk the egg yolks and add them to the melted chocolate, whisking until blended. Stir in the rum, bourbon, or liqueur.

3. In a clean bowl, beat the egg whites at high speed until they form soft peaks. Gradually add the sugar and continue to beat at high speed until the meringue forms stiff peaks.

4. Whisk one third of the meringue into the chocolate mixture to lighten it. Fold in the remaining whites.

5. Beat the cream until stiff and fold it into the chocolate mixture a third at a time.

6. Cover and refrigerate the mousse until firm. This mousse keeps well for 3 to 5 days, and may be frozen for up to 1 week.

∎

Poured Fondant

Poured over a cake, fondant looks satiny, smooth, and shiny. Porcelain white or delicately tinted to pale pastel, fondant provides that pearly finish so characteristic of wedding cakes and classic petits fours. Covering a cake with fondant seals in moisture so that the cake will stay fresh for a few days without refrigeration.

Traditional fondant is a mixture of water, sugar, and corn syrup that is heated to a high temperature and then kneaded with a pastry scraper as it cools so that it develops a satin-like sheen and perfectly smooth consistency. As it's hard to make at home and is easily available through a number of specialty stores and bakers' supply houses (see Sources of Supply) many bakers prefer to buy fondant.

Before pouring fondant, the cake should be frosted with a thin coating of buttercream or preserves, which seals the cake and provides the fondant with a smooth base. If you are using buttercream, chill the cake before pouring on the fondant, which can melt and discolor room temperature buttercream.

The fondant is heated to a pourable consistency in a double boiler set over water that has been heated to about 150°. Place the double boiler over very low heat and stir the melting fondant up from the bottom with a rubber spatula. Keep the fondant in motion while it melts so that it will be as smooth as possible. Poured fondant should be thinned with a little stock syrup or water so that it is liquid. Set a candy thermometer in the pan and heat the fondant to 95°.

Position the cake on a wire rack set over a shallow pan and pour the heated fondant over the center of the cake, just as you would any glaze. Use a flexible metal spatula to smooth the fondant over the cake in those areas that are not already covered. Work quickly as the fondant sets almost at once. When the fondant has hardened slightly, trim around the bottom of the cake with a sharp paring knife. Let the cake sit at room temperature until you are ready to decorate and serve.

■

Rolled Fondant

Rolled fondant, which is easily made at home, is a mixture of confectioners' sugar, corn syrup, glycerine, water, and gelatin. It has a matte finish rather than a shiny one and is handled very differently from poured fondant. First roll it out on a board dusted with confectioners' sugar. Next, slip your hands, palms down, under the rolled fondant and center it over the cake. Smooth the fondant in place, gently patting it to remove the wrinkles and creases.

Rolled fondant may be used instead of pastillage. In this case, the fondant shapes need to be dried for 24 to 48 hours to achieve adequate rigidity. Because the fondant absorbs the sugar, it may become too stiff. In this case, add a small amount of water and rework it.

Makes enough to cover a two-layer 10-inch cake
Preparation time 20 to 25 minutes

¼ cup cold water

1 tablespoon gelatin

½ cup light corn syrup

1 tablespoon (½ ounce) glycerine

1 teaspoon clear extract

Liquid food coloring (optional)

2 pounds plus 1 cup confectioners' sugar

1. Pour the ¼ cup cold water into a small saucepan. Sprinkle the gelatin on top and allow it to soften for about 5 minutes. Place over low heat and stir until the gelatin is completely dissolved— about 15 to 20 seconds.

2. Stir in the corn syrup, glycerine, extract, and food coloring.

3. Place 2 pounds of confectioners' sugar in the bowl of an electric mixer. Add the gelatin mixture and, using the paddle attachment if you have one, beat until the mixture is thick and doughlike. If it is too stiff, add water a tablespoon at a time. Turn the fondant out on a work surface that has been dusted with confectioners' sugar. Knead by

hand until the fondant holds its shape and is not tacky—1 to 2 minutes.

4. Roll the fondant to ⅓-inch thickness to drape a cake, or cut according to the cake you are making.

5. Leftover fondant may be wrapped in plastic and stored in the refrigerator for up to two weeks.

■

Fruit Glaze

A warm, glistening glaze is quick and delicious.

Makes ¾ cup
Preparation time 10 minutes

12 ounces apricot or raspberry preserves, or 1 pint currant jelly

1. Place the preserves or jelly in a heavy saucepan. Bring to boil over medium heat, stirring occasionally with a wooden spoon.

2. Strain into another saucepan and bring to a boil once more. Remove from heat and immediately pour over the cake.

3. Any unused glaze may be refrigerated, tightly covered, for 2 to 3 weeks.

■

Stock Syrup

Stock syrups flavored with liqueurs moisten large cake layers before filling. Stored in a tightly covered container, stock syrup keeps indefinitely.

Makes 1½ cups
Preparation time 10 minutes

½ cup water

1 cup sugar

1. Combine water and sugar in a small saucepan and bring to a boil over medium heat.

2. Cook until the sugar has completely dissolved—about 1 or 2 minutes. Cool before using.

3. Stock syrup may be flavored with liqueur. Add 2 to 3 tablespoons when the syrup cools.

■

Praline

One of the underrated heroes of baking, praline is simply sugar melted to the point when it caramelizes, with almonds or hazelnuts added at the last minute. Spread on a baking sheet, praline hardens into a crunchy, nutty candy. It can be broken into large pieces to use as a decoration or finely ground for flavoring buttercream or sprinkling between layers.

Makes 1⅔ cups
Preparation time 15 to 20 minutes

1 cup sugar

⅓ cup whole or sliced almonds or toasted, skinned hazelnuts

1. Generously butter a baking sheet or marble slab.

2. Place the sugar in a 1-quart, heavy bottom saucepan over medium heat. Do not stir until the sugar starts to change color. Stir with a wooden spoon until the sugar melts and turns amber, 4 to 6 minutes. Remove from the heat and continue stirring. The caramel will continue to cook even after it has been taken from the heat.

3. Quickly stir the nuts into the caramel. Immediately pour the praline onto the baking sheet or marble.

4. When the praline is cold and hard, loosen it from the pan with a metal spatula. Break it into pieces or crush it finely in a food processor. The praline may be stored in an airtight jar but should not be refrigerated. If the praline solidifies, it can be reground.

■

Candied Citrus Peel

Tart and crunchy, candied peel adds color and texture to a variety of cakes.

Makes 2 cups
Preparation time 1½ to 2 hours

2 cups thin strips of grapefruit, orange, lime, or lemon peel

1 cup sugar

1 cup confectioners' sugar, optional

1. Place the citrus peel in a heavy saucepan. Cover with 1½ cups of cold water and bring to a boil over medium heat. Drain the peel thoroughly. Cover with another 1½ cups of cold water and repeat. Blanch the peel another time.

2. Place the sugar and 1 cup of water in a saucepan and bring to a boil, stirring until the sugar is dissolved. Add the peel and boil until the syrup thickens and the peel is transparent, about 15 to 20 minutes.

3. Roll the peel in confectioners' sugar if desired and spread on racks to dry.

4. Store the candied peel in an airtight container.

■

Pastillage

Pastillage must be wrapped in plastic and a damp towel or stored in an airtight container at all times, since exposure to air will make it dry out and harden. Therefore, do read the directions carefully before beginning so that you can work quickly and efficiently. When working with pastillage, break off only the amount you need and keep the rest covered. Use cornstarch on the rolling pin and work surface, and keep work area, hands, and tools clean at all times, as pastillage will pick up any trace of dirt. Always make extra pastillage petals or leaves to allow for breakage.

Makes 2 cups
Preparation time 10 to 15 minutes, plus 1 hour resting time

½ tablespoon powdered gelatin

1 pound confectioners' sugar

Pinch cream of tartar

½ cup cornstarch

1. Measure 3 tablespoons of water into a small bowl and sprinkle gelatin over the water. Let the mixture sit for 2 to 3 minutes until the gelatin "blooms" (absorbs the water).

2. Place the bowl over hot water until the gelatin melts and becomes somewhat clear, about 3 minutes.

3. Combine the sugar, cream of tartar, and cornstarch in a large bowl of an electric mixer. Do not use an aluminum bowl as this will turn the pastillage gray. Mix on low speed and add the gelatin. Continue mixing until the ingredients are combined. The "dough" should completely come away from the sides of the bowl. If it is too sticky, work more sugar into it. If the mixture is too dry and crumbly, add a few drops of water until it starts developing a smoother consistency.

4. Remove the pastillage from the bowl. Knead it as you would marzipan or bread dough, using cornstarch as necessary to keep it from sticking to the work surface until it becomes very white and smooth, about 3 minutes. Wrap the pastillage in plastic wrap and cover with a damp towel. Store in the refrigerator for at least 1 hour.

5. Unwrap and test the consistency of the pastillage. It should be pliable, like bread dough. If it is too loose, knead in some confectioners' sugar, a little at a time, until the pastillage becomes pliable.

6. Roll the pastillage to a thickness of about ¹⁄₁₆ inch and proceed according to the directions for the decoration you are making.

ORANGE CAKE WITH ICED FRUIT

Recipe, Page 38

CHAPTER THREE

■

Spring & Summer

ORANGE CAKE WITH ICED FRUIT

Photograph, Page 36
Orange Layer Cake flavored with Cointreau or Grand Marnier, filled with Orange Buttercream and marmalade, frosted with Orange Buttercream, and decorated with fresh fruit and Candied Orange Peel.
Serves 8 to 10

Fresh fruit is one of the simplest and most dramatic decorations, adding a rich palette of textures and colors to the design while also appearing light and fresh. Here the fruit has been made more alluring with a sugar frosting and its qualities underlined by the simplicity of the buttercream frosting.

EQUIPMENT

Two 8-inch round pans

WORK PLAN

Up to 1 day ahead—
Bake the Orange Layer Cake and prepare the iced fruit, Candied Orange Peel, and Orange Buttercream.
Baking & Preparation—
About 3 hours
Assembly & Decoration—
About 1 hour, including chilling time

RECIPE

Seasonal fruit—grapes, large strawberries with stems, and blackberries

1 egg white

1½ cups sugar

1 recipe Candied Orange Peel, Page 35

1 recipe Orange Layer Cake, Page 22

1 recipe Orange Buttercream, Page 28

1 to 2 tablespoons Cointreau or Grand Marnier

2 to 3 tablespoons bitter orange marmalade

PREPARATION

1. At least 3 hours ahead, prepare the iced fruit. Gently wash and dry the fruit. Whisk the egg white with a fork until foamy. Dip the fruit in the egg white and let the excess run off. Dust the fruit with sugar, or gently roll in a 1 inch deep layer of sugar. Handling the fruit carefully, set on a rack to dry for several hours or overnight.

2. Make the candied peel.

3. Bake the cake in two 8-inch round pans. Prepare the buttercream.

ASSEMBLY & DECORATION

4. When the cake layers are cool, place one on a flat serving plate or a cardboard round. Sprinkle with liqueur and then spread with the marmalade. With a metal spatula, spread about ½ cup of buttercream over the marmalade and top with the second cake layer. Smooth any buttercream that has seeped out between the layers, and refrigerate until the filling sets—15 to 30 minutes.

5. Frost the cake with half the remaining buttercream, beginning with the sides and ending with the top, as described on page 13. Refrigerate 15 to 30 minutes more.

6. Frost the cake again with buttercream. Refrigerate the cake for 15 to 30 minutes, or until ready to decorate.

7. Group the sugar-dipped fruits on top of the cake. Begin with larger fruits, in this case a bunch of green grapes, placed near the top edge of the cake. Place a small cluster of grapes or several berries at the base of the cake. Drop strips of candied peel randomly over the fruit and over the top and sides of the cake.

STORING & SERVING

The cake can be assembled and decorated up to 4 hours in advance and kept in the refrigerator; remove 1 hour before serving.

PICNIC NUT CAKE

Photograph, Page 40
Pound Cake flavored with Frangelico, filled and frosted
with apricot preserves, and decorated with Brazil nuts,
raspberries, and mint leaves. Serves 6 to 8

Often overlooked by decorators in favor of almonds and pecans, Brazil nuts nevertheless bring a distinctive flavor and texture to a cake, and as they are used here, add a sculptural quality as well. If raspberries aren't available, they can be replaced with blueberries or blackberries, and sprigs of lemon thyme can substitute for mint leaves. Easy and quick to decorate, this cake is a good traveler.

EQUIPMENT

One 6-inch round pan, 4 inches deep

WORK PLAN

Up to 1 day ahead—
Bake the Pound Cake.
Baking & Preparation—
About 1¼ hours
Assembly & Decoration—
About ½ hour

RECIPE

1 recipe Pound Cake, Page 23

½ pint raspberries

About 30 mint leaves

¼ cup Frangelico

8 ounces apricot preserves

1 pound shelled Brazil nuts

PREPARATION

1. Bake the cake in a 6-inch round pan. Wash and dry raspberries and mint leaves.

ASSEMBLY & DECORATION

2. When the cake is cool, slice it into three layers, using a long serrated knife. Sprinkle each layer with Frangelico. Set one layer on a cardboard round or flat serving plate. With a metal spatula, spread the first layer with 2 tablespoons of apricot preserves, top with a second layer, and spread with more preserves. Top with the third layer. Spread the remaining preserves evenly over the sides and top of the cake.

3. Press the nuts first over the sides and then the top of the cake so that it is completely covered. Fill in any gaps along the top edge or sides with more nuts. If nuts do not adhere to a spot on the cake, apply a dab of extra preserves to secure them.

4. Garnish the top with six to eight evenly spaced raspberries, setting them in the crevices between the nuts. You may have to lift off a nut here and there and replace it so that the berry is held firmly in place. Tuck two mint leaves under each raspberry. Arrange several clusters of raspberries at equal distances around the base of the cake and to finish, add mint leaves at the sides of each cluster.

STORING & SERVING

Without the raspberry and mint leaf garnish, the cake can sit at room temperature or under a cake dome for up to 1 day. If you want to make it more than a day before serving, store the cake in the refrigerator and let it come to room temperature before garnishing.

PICNIC NUT CAKE
·
Recipe, Page 39

FLUTED POUND CAKE WITH BERRY PUREE

Photograph, Page 44
Pound Cake dusted with confectioners' sugar surrounded
by raspberry and blackberry purees and garnished with
fresh berries. Serves 6 to 8

For its simplicity and versatility, stenciling is justly popular with bakers. It needs only a paper template and a dusting of confectioners' sugar or cocoa to make a cake softly elegant or boldly geometric; and frequently this need be the only decoration.

In this recipe, the pound cake is baked in a fluted pan. But a heatproof gelatin mold, charlotte mold, or a loaf pan can equally be used and the stencil altered to suit the shape of the cake.

EQUIPMENT

One fluted pan 5- to 6-inches across,
4- to 5-inches deep
Parchment paper
Fine sieve
Tweezers

WORK PLAN

Up to 2 days ahead—
Bake the Pound Cake and prepare the berry purees.
Baking & Preparation—
About 1¼ hours
Assembly & Decoration—
About ½ hour

RECIPE

1 recipe Pound Cake, Page 23

½ pint raspberries

1 tablespoon raspberry preserves

½ pint blackberries

1 tablespoon blackberry preserves

1 cup confectioners' sugar

PREPARATION

1. Bake the cake in a 5- to 6-inch fluted pan.

2. Wash and dry the berries. Reserve a few of each for garnish. Place the rest of the raspberries and the raspberry jam in a food processor or blender and puree. Sieve the puree to remove the seeds. Repeat with the blackberries and blackberry preserves. Set aside in separate bowls.

ASSEMBLY & DECORATION

3. When the cake is cool, set it on a serving plate. Place strips of paper around the cake to catch the excess sifted sugar. Cut 5 pieces of parchment paper to use as stencils: 1 square piece, 1 to 1½-inch square, and 4 teardrop-shaped pieces, about 2 inches long. Use the cake itself to gauge exactly how large to cut the stencils. Place the stencils on top of the cake and dust with confectioners' sugar.

4. Spoon the pureed berries around the cake, alternating the raspberry with the blackberry. Garnish with the reserved whole berries.

Stenciling a Cake

Holding a sieve about 6 inches above the cake, sift the confectioners' sugar over the top. Be careful not to move the sieve quickly as a draft will smudge the pattern. Remove the stencil with tweezers and discard the paper around the cake.

STORING & SERVING

The cake should be served within the hour after assembling.

SUMMER FRUIT ROULADE

Photograph, Page 45
Genoise flavored with framboise or kirsch, filled with
sweetened crème fraîche and summer fruits, frosted
with sweetened crème fraîche, and decorated with
summer fruit and lemon leaves. Serves 8 to 10

Rolled cakes, or roulades, are deceptively easy to assemble and always charming. When making a roulade, roll the cake while it is still warm and flexible, before filling. Once it has cooled, the cake can be unrolled, filled, and rolled again.

The cake in the photograph required 6 red and purple plums, 8 cherries, 2 kiwi, 1 peach, and ½ cup of blackberries, but the selection can be varied according to availability and preference. If you fill the cake more than two hours before serving, sprinkle the sliced fruit with the juice of ½ lemon before rolling the cake to prevent discoloration.

Commercial crème fraîche is recommended here because when it is whipped to stiff peaks, store-bought holds up better than homemade.

EQUIPMENT

One 11½- by 15½-inch jelly roll pan
Parchment paper or kitchen towel

WORK PLAN

Up to 1 day ahead—
Bake the Genoise.
Up to 2 hours ahead—
Prepare the crème fraîche and slice the fruit.
Baking & Preparation—
About 1 hour
Assembly & Decoration—
About 2 hours, including chilling time

RECIPE

1 recipe Genoise, Page 20

½ cup confectioners' sugar

Seasonal fruit—plums, cherries, kiwi, peaches,
blackberries

2 cups crème fraîche

2 to 4 tablespoons framboise or kirsch

Lemon leaves

PREPARATION

1. Bake the genoise in a jelly roll pan. While the cake is still slightly warm, place a piece of parchment paper or a clean kitchen towel that is one or two inches longer than the cake on a work surface. Dust the paper or towel with 2 tablespoons of confectioners' sugar. Carefully turn the cake out onto the paper or towel and sprinkle 2 tablespoons of confectioners' sugar over the surface. Roll the cake and allow to cool completely.

2. Wash and dry the fruit and leaves. Cut a few of the larger fruits into thin slices and combine with enough berries to make 2 cups. Reserve the best-looking fruits for garnish.

3. In an electric mixer at medium speed, whip the crème fraîche with the remaining ¼ cup confectioners' sugar just until stiff peaks form. Do not overwhip or the cream may break down. Refrigerate until ready to use.

ASSEMBLY & DECORATION

4. To fill the roulade, carefully unroll the cooled cake on the parchment paper or towel. Sprinkle it with the liqueur. With a metal spatula, spread 1 to 1½ cups of the sweetened crème fraîche over the cake. Arrange the fruit in a thin layer on the cream, spaced about ¼ inch apart. Roll the cake again, using your fingers and the parchment paper to make the roll as compact as possible. Discard the paper or towel, and gently lift the roulade, seam side down, on to a serving plate by hand or with a metal spatula. Chill the cake and the remaining crème fraîche for 20 to 30 minutes.

5. Frost the cake again with crème fraîche and chill the cake for 15 to 30 minutes.

6. Smooth the frosting with a metal spatula. Using a sharp knife, cut a thin slice off each end of the roulade to form a neat, clean edge and expose some of the filling. Press lemon leaves into the sides of the cake. Garnish the platter with leaves and sliced and whole fruits.

Rolling a Cake

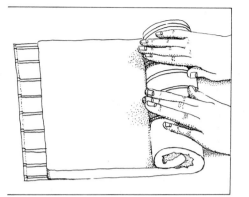

Using the parchment paper or cloth as an aid, roll the warm cake along the short side into a fairly tight roll. Set the cake aside to cool completely.

STORING & SERVING

The decorated cake should be refrigerated for several hours but should sit at room temperature for 30 minutes before serving.

INTERMEDIATE

STRAWBERRY CREAM CAKE

Photograph, Page 48
Yellow Layer Cake filled with sweetened whipped cream and berries, frosted with whipped cream and crème fraîche, and decorated with fresh strawberries, raspberries, blueberries, and blackberries. Serves 8 to 10

To brighten the cream that decorates this delicious summer layer cake to a delicate pink color, a little raspberry puree is folded in after whipping. The puree also adds a tart accent to the cream, which offsets some of its richness, although you may have to increase the amount of sugar if the raspberries are not very sweet.

EQUIPMENT

Two 8-inch round pans
Ateco #5 round tip
Pastry bag

WORK PLAN

Up to 1 day ahead—
Bake the Yellow Layer Cake.
Up to 2 hours before serving—
Prepare the whipped cream, trim the fruit, and make the puree.
Baking & Preparation—
About 1 hour
Assembly & Decoration—
About 45 minutes, including chilling time

RECIPE

1 recipe Yellow Layer Cake, Page 22

1 pint raspberries

½ pint blueberries

1¼ pints blackberries

1½ pints strawberries

1½ cups heavy cream

½ cup crème fraîche

3 to 4 tablespoons sugar

PREPARATION

1. Bake the cake in two 8-inch round pans.

2. Wash and dry the berries. Puree half the raspberries in a food processor or blender. Sieve to remove the seeds.

3. To prepare the sweetened whipped cream, pour the creams into the bowl of an electric mixer and add 3 tablespoons of sugar. Whip the cream at medium speed until it forms very soft peaks. With a rubber spatula, gently fold in the raspberry puree. Taste for sweetness and add more sugar if necessary. Continue beating the cream just until it forms stiff peaks.

4. Reserve six strawberries for the top of the cake and slice them in half lengthwise, leaving the hulls. Similarly, reserve about twenty blueberries, six raspberries, and one blackberry and set aside with the strawberries. Combine the remaining berries with the sliced strawberries.

FLUTED POUND CAKE WITH BERRY PUREE

Recipe, Page 41

SUMMER FRUIT ROULADE
·
Recipe, Page 42

ASSEMBLY & DECORATION

5. When the cake layers are cool, place one on a flat serving plate or cardboard round. With a metal spatula, spread the layer with about ½ cup of whipped cream. Arrange a layer of the mixed berries over the cream. Spread another ½ cup of whipped cream over the fruit and position the second cake layer on top.

6. Frost the cake with whipped cream, beginning with the sides and ending with the top. Refrigerate the cake and cream for 15 to 30 minutes.

7. Spoon whipped cream into a pastry bag fitted with a #5 tip. Pipe the columns around the side of the cake. Use a sharp knife or metal spatula to smooth the tops of the columns so that they are level with the top of the cake.

8. Arrange the strawberries on top of the cake in a concentric pattern, as in the photograph. Still using the #5 tip, pipe a bead border around the top of the cake. Use the same tip to pipe a circle of large beads around the tips of the berries. Place a blackberry in the center of the cake. Surround with a circle of raspberries and then a circle of blueberries.

Piping Bead Borders & Columns

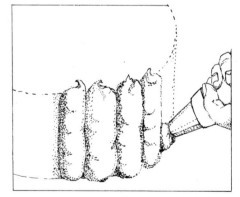

Holding the bag at a 45-degree angle to the side of the cake, pipe each vertical column with a single upward stroke.

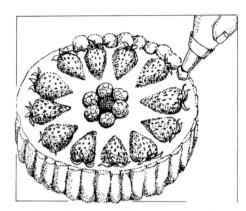

Pipe a bead border around the top of the cake, covering the tops of the columns. Use the same tip to pipe a circle of large beads around the tips of the berries.

STORING & SERVING

Refrigerate the cake for up to 3 or 4 hours, and allow it to sit at room temperature for 15 minutes before serving.

INTERMEDIATE

STRAWBERRY TRIFLE

Photograph, Page 49
Chocolate Layer Cake sprinkled with Grand Marnier, filled with sweetened whipped cream and crème fraîche and strawberries, frosted with Ganache, and decorated with strawberries and chocolate ribbons.
Serves 12 to 14

Dark chocolate and fresh strawberries are a pairing that seems made in heaven. Much of the success of this cake depends on aligning the fruit between the layers precisely and marking the positions of the outer rows carefully on parchment paper so that the berries are cut cleanly through their centers.

As the cake bakes, it may rise in the center; it will level off as it cools. You will have some ganache left over from this recipe which can be stored in the refrigerator for several days for later use.

EQUIPMENT

One 11½- by 15½-inch jelly roll pan
Parchment paper
Cardboard

WORK PLAN

Up to 1 day ahead—
Bake the Chocolate Layer Cake and prepare the Ganache and chocolate ribbons.
Up to 2 hours before serving—
Prepare the whipped cream and trim the strawberries.
Baking & Preparation—
About 2 hours
Assembly & Decoration—
About 1½ hours, including chilling time

RECIPE

1 recipe Chocolate Layer Cake, Page 22

½ recipe Ganache, Page 29

4 ounces semisweet chocolate

¼ cup Grand Marnier

1 cup crème fraîche

¾ cup heavy cream

1 to 2 tablespoons sugar

2½ pints large strawberries

PREPARATION

1. Bake the cake in a jelly roll pan. Prepare the ganache.

2. Make the chocolate ribbons. Melt and spread the chocolate following the instructions on page 70, spreading this smaller quantity over a smaller area. Refrigerate the chocolate until set, then scrape into long, narrow ribbons.

3. Trim the stem ends from the large strawberries.

ASSEMBLY & DECORATION

4. When the cake is cool, place it on a flat surface. Trim off the edges, using a long serrated knife. Cut the cake in half lengthwise to make two 4- by 13-inch strips. Cut a piece of parchment paper slightly bigger than the cake and place on a cardboard rectangle cut to fit the cake. Center one cake layer on the parchment and sprinkle with half the Grand Marnier.

5. In an electric mixer, beat the crème fraîche and the heavy cream with 1 tablespoon of sugar at high speed just until it forms stiff peaks. Add more sugar to taste. Do not overbeat.

6. With a metal spatula, spread a thin coating of whipped cream over the top of the moistened cake layer.

7. Place the strawberries on the cream in straight rows, with the pointed tips upward. Line the strawberries along all four edges of the cake; do not leave a border. To indicate where to trim the cake, mark the parchment paper at the centers of the end, outside strawberries to indicate where to trim the cake.

8. With a small knife, spread another layer of whipped cream over the berries, pressing it down gently to fill in the gaps between the berries. All but the tips of the tallest berries should be covered.

9. Gently position the second strip of cake on top of the berries and cream. Sprinkle with the remaining Grand Marnier. Spread a thin layer of ganache over the top of the cake. Refrigerate for 20 to 30 minutes to set.

10. When the frosting is firm, spread another layer of ganache over the top of the cake.

11. With a serrated knife, neatly trim each side of the cake, using the marks on the parchment paper as a guide so that you cut neatly through the centers of all four outside rows of berries. Hold the knife at a 45-degree angle to the cake and cut through the bottom of the cake with clean, steady strokes. Apply pressure on the downstrokes, touching the tip of the knife to the parchment each time. Do not "saw" the cake.

12. Transfer the cake to a serving plate. Decorate the top of the cake with chocolate ribbons and strawberries. Garnish the base of the cake with chocolate ribbons.

SERVING & STORING

Refrigerate cake until 30 minutes before serving. If it's made more than 2 hours in advance, it should be loosely covered with plastic wrap.

To serve, cut slices across the width of the cake, guiding the knife between the berries.

STRAWBERRY CREAM CAKE

Recipe, Page 43

STRAWBERRY TRIFLE
.
Recipe, Page 46

GENOISE BASKET WITH RASPBERRIES

Photograph, Page 52
Coffee Genoise filled and frosted with Coffee Buttercream
and decorated with fresh raspberries. Serves 6 to 8

A favorite of cake decorators, the classic basket weave decorating technique is often seen around buttercream wedding cakes. Formed with just two tips, it is not at all difficult to master, and it is one of the most effective techniques for a less experienced decorator to use. Here, paired with a basket-shaped cake, it creates a witty container for a harvest of fresh raspberries (or blueberries, blackberries, or strawberries).

EQUIPMENT

Two 8-inch round pans
Ateco #5 and #8 round and #48 basket weave tips
One or two pastry bags

WORK PLAN

Up to 1 day ahead—
Bake the Coffee Genoise and prepare the Coffee Buttercream.
Baking & Preparation—
About 1¼ hours
Assembly & Decoration—
About 1½ hours, including chilling time

RECIPE

1 recipe Coffee Genoise, Page 21

1 recipe Coffee Buttercream, Page 28

2 pints fresh raspberries

PREPARATION

1. Bake the genoise in two 8-inch round pans and prepare the buttercream. Wash and dry the raspberries.

2. To trim the cake, cut an 8-inch oval template for the shape of the basket from parchment paper.

ASSEMBLY & DECORATION

3. When the genoise layers have cooled, set one layer on a turntable or cardboard round. Place the template on the cake and mark around the edge with a toothpick. Carefully trim the layer, using a serrated knife, into an 8-inch oval. Repeat with the second layer. (For more information on trimming cakes, see page 12.) With a long serrated knife, slice both ovals in half horizontally so that you have four layers altogether.

4. Place one layer on the turntable or cardboard round. With a metal spatula, spread the layer with about ½ cup of buttercream. Place a second layer on top and spread with ½ cup of buttercream. Add a third layer and frost, then top with the fourth layer. Refrigerate the cake until the filling has set—15 to 30 minutes.

5. When the filling is firm, frost the cake with buttercream, beginning with the sides and ending with the top. Refrigerate the cake for 15 to 20 minutes.

6. Spoon buttercream into a pastry bag and attach a #8 tip. Pipe vertical lines ¼ to ½ inch apart up the sides of the cake. Replace the tip with a #48 tip. Pipe rows of basket weave strips alternately over every other vertical line. Refrigerate the cake again for 15 to 20 minutes.

7. Using a long metal spatula, carefully transfer the cake to a serving plate. Attach a #5 tip to the pastry bag. Pipe an elongated bead border around the base of the basket, drawing the bag slightly to the right of the base of each bead to extend it. Then pipe a border around the top by piping beads at alternating angles, pivoting your wrists as you change the position of the bag to create a feathered effect. Refrigerate to set the decoration.

8. Just before serving, heap the raspberries on top of the cake and cluster a few at the base of the basket.

Piping a Basket Weave

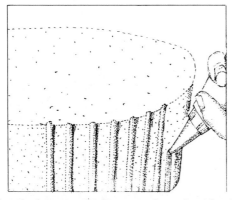

Holding the bag at a 45-degree angle to the side of the cake and applying gentle pressure, pipe slim vertical lines with a #8 tip at ¼- to ½-inch intervals from the base to the top of the cake.

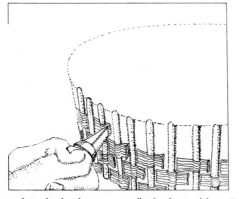

To complete the basket weave, fit the bag with a #48 tip. Hold the bag at a 90-degree angle to the cake and pipe a row of basket weave around the cake. To achieve the basket effect, pipe over every other vertical line, and alternate each row.

STORING & SERVING

Refrigerate the cake for up to 4 hours, and allow it to sit at room temperature for 30 minutes before serving.

LEMON ROSE CAKE

Photograph, Page 53
Lemon Genoise filled with Lemon Buttercream, blueberries, and blueberry preserves, frosted with Lemon Buttercream, and decorated with buttercream roses.
Serves 8 to 10

The techniques for the roses and borders that decorate this lemon genoise, though different in nature, depend similarly on having buttercream at the right temperature and consistency, and a steady hand.

The roses are piped onto a flower "nail"—a nail on which a slightly domed metal disk has been soldered—that is available at cake decorating supply stores. A core of frosting is piped first, and the petals are added one at a time, beginning with the center ones, using a pastry bag fitted with a rose petal tip. If your first roses look more like carnations, persevere and practice—it's largely a matter of learning to control your hand movements and the pressure on the bag.

To position the rhythmic swirls of the border regularly, or indeed any pattern on a cake, make tiny marks on the frosted cake to indicate where the design changes. As you pipe around the cake, the marks will be covered.

EQUIPMENT

Two 8-inch round pans
Ateco #31 star, #70 leaf, and #104 petal tips
Two pastry bags
Flower nail
Waxed paper

WORK PLAN

Up to 1 day ahead—
Bake the Lemon Genoise and prepare the Lemon Buttercream. Pipe the buttercream roses.
Baking & Preparation—
About 1¼ hours
Assembly & Decoration—
About 2 hours, including chilling time

RECIPE

1 recipe Lemon Genoise, Page 21

1 recipe Lemon Buttercream, Page 28

GENOISE BASKET WITH RASPBERRIES
·
Recipe, Page 50

LEMON ROSE CAKE
·
Recipe, Page 51

½ recipe Swiss Meringue Buttercream, Page 27

¼ cup blueberry preserves

½ pint blueberries

Yellow and green food coloring

PREPARATION

1. Bake the genoise in two 8-inch round pans. Prepare the buttercreams and tint each pale yellow.

ASSEMBLY & DECORATION

2. When the genoise layers are cool, place one layer on a cardboard round or flat serving plate. Using a metal spatula, spread with about ½ cup of buttercream. Spread the blueberry preserves over the buttercream. Arrange a layer of the blueberries over the preserves. Place the second layer on top, and smooth any filling that may have seeped out. Refrigerate the cake until the filling sets—15 to 30 minutes.

3. Reserve the Swiss meringue buttercream for decoration. Frost the cake with half the lemon buttercream, beginning with the sides and ending with the top. Refrigerate the cake again for 15 to 20 minutes.

4. Frost the cake a second time, using the metal spatula warmed in hot water and then dried for a smooth finish. Refrigerate the cake until ready to decorate.

5. Make the four buttercream roses on a rose nail. Before beginning each rose, affix a small square of waxed paper to the nail with a dab of buttercream. Fit a #104 tip in a pastry bag and fill the bag with buttercream. Pipe the roses according to the illustrations. Refrigerate the roses on a plate or baking sheet for 15 minutes.

6. For the border, mark the frosting where the piping elongates and the pattern changes. Pipe the border with a #3 tip.

7. Color ½ cup of buttercream to a soft green. Spoon the buttercream into a pastry bag and fit with a #70 tip. Pipe the leaves on top of the cake following the illustration. Reserve a little of the green buttercream for extra leaves.

8. Position the roses on the cake by lifting them from the waxed paper with a metal spatula and setting them on the leaves. Pipe one or two more leaves onto the cake between the roses.

Piping Buttercream Roses & Leaves

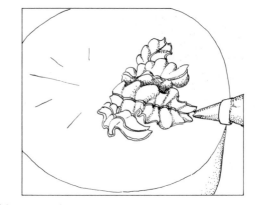

With a #70 tip, pipe the leaves on top of the cake beginning with two long leaves about 2 inches apart on opposite sides of the top. Pipe two smaller leaves on each side of these.

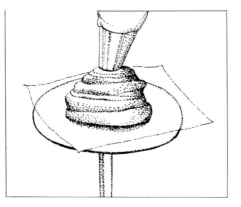

Fix a small square of waxed paper on top of the nail, using a dab of buttercream. With a #104 tip, pipe the core of the rose, about ½ inch high, on the center of the nail. To support the petals, the core should be symmetrical and balanced.

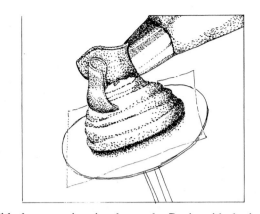

With the same tip, pipe the petals. Begin with the inside petals, piped near the top of the core. Hold the bag at a 45-degree angle to the core and pipe with medium pressure. Rotate the nail between your fingers as you pipe the petals around the core.

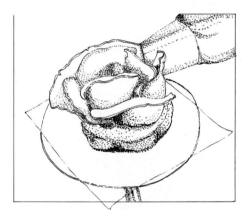

Pipe the outer petals, twisting the bag so that the petals are flared out from the center of the rose. As each rose is completed, remove it from the nail by lifting the waxed paper.

STORING & SERVING

The decorated cake may be stored in the refrigerator for several hours, but should sit at room temperature for 30 minutes before serving.

DARK CHOCOLATE TRUFFLE CAKE
·
Recipe, Page 58

CHAPTER FOUR

■

Fall & Winter

DARK CHOCOLATE TRUFFLE CAKE

Photograph, Page 56
Dense Chocolate Cake frosted with Butter Ganache and
decorated with cocoa truffles, chocolate twigs,
and cocoa. Serves 8 to 10

A sophisticated finale for a special dinner party, this dramatic chocolate cake is almost ridiculously simple to decorate. Store-bought cocoa truffles and chocolate twigs are arranged on the cake and lightly dusted with cocoa—five minutes! Chocolate twigs are available in specialty shops or through the mail from Universal Foods (see Sources of Supply, page 188). Truffles, of course, are sold in candy stores. The choice of centers is up to you, but we recommend plain truffles rolled in cocoa, rather than chocolate-dipped.

EQUIPMENT

One 8-inch round springform pan

WORK PLAN

Up to 2 days ahead—
Bake the Dense Chocolate Cake and prepare the Butter Ganache.
Baking & Preparation—
About 1 hour
Assembly & Decoration—
About ¾ hour, including chilling time

RECIPE

1 recipe Dense Chocolate Cake, Page 26

½ recipe Butter Ganache, Page 30

2 tablespoons unsweetened cocoa

10 or 12 cocoa truffles

12 or 15 chocolate twigs

PREPARATION

1. Bake the cake in an 8-inch round springform pan. Prepare the ganache.

ASSEMBLY & DECORATION

2. When the cake is cool, invert it on a flat serving plate or cardboard round. With a metal spatula, frost the cake with half the ganache, beginning with the sides and ending with the top. (For detailed frosting instructions, see page 13.) Refrigerate the cake for 15 to 20 minutes.

3. Frost the cake a second time with the remaining ganache. Finish the frosting with a metal spatula warmed in hot water and then dried. Refrigerate the cake until ready to decorate.

4. Sift a tablespoon of cocoa over the center of the cake. Pile the truffles in an asymmetrical pattern slightly off-center. Arrange the twigs over and around the truffles. Sift more cocoa over the truffles and twigs.

STORING & SERVING

The cake can be served immediately. If it is to be kept for several hours, it should be refrigerated until 30 minutes before serving. Because the ganache could absorb the cocoa, decorate the cake no more than 2 or 3 hours before serving. Cut this very rich cake into thin slices.

RICH PISTACHIO CAKE

Photograph, Page 60
Chocolate Layer Cake filled with Ganache and ground
pistachios, frosted with Ganache, and decorated with
whole pistachios. Serves 8 to 10

With chocolate and pistachios on hand, this cake can be baked and decorated in just a couple of hours and is an ideal choice for last-minute entertaining. Pistachios are an unusual and interesting selection for decorating a cake; we opted for natural pistachios, but red ones will add their bright color.

EQUIPMENT

Two 8-inch round pans

WORK PLAN

Up to 1 day ahead—
Bake the Chocolate Layer Cake, and prepare the Ganache.
Baking & Preparation—
About 1 hour
Assembly & Decoration—
About 1 hour, including chilling time

RECIPE

1 recipe Chocolate Layer Cake, Page 22

1 recipe Ganache, Page 30

½ pound unsalted pistachios

PREPARATION

1. Bake the cake in two 8-inch round pans. Prepare the ganache and allow it to cool.

2. Shell and finely grind 2 ounces of pistachios in a nut grinder or food processor.

ASSEMBLY & DECORATION

3. When the cake layers are cool, whip the ganache until it becomes thick enough to spread and lightens in color. Place one cake layer on a flat serving plate or cardboard round. With a metal spatula, spread about ½ cup of ganache over the cake. Sprinkle the ground pistachios over the ganache and position the second layer on top. Smooth any ganache that may have seeped out between the layers and refrigerate the cake until the filling sets—15 to 30 minutes.

4. If the ganache has hardened, rewhip it in the electric mixer with the paddle attachment, if you have one. Frost the cake with half the remaining ganache, beginning with the sides and ending with the top. (For detailed frosting instructions, see page 13.) Refrigerate the cake again for 15 to 20 minutes.

5. Frost the cake again. To give the frosting a smooth finish, use a metal spatula that has been warmed in hot water, then dried.

6. Reserve eighteen to twenty pistachios in their shells. Shell the remaining nuts and set aside several whole ones. Coarsely chop most of the nuts, and finely chop the rest. Decorate the cake by gently pressing coarsely chopped and whole pistachios around the base and top. Pull apart some of the shells and leave others nearly closed. Add random clusters of unshelled nuts on the pistachio border and at the base of the cake. Sprinkle four strips of the finely ground pistachios on top of the cake, and set two or three unshelled pistachios in the center.

STORING & SERVING

The cake may be refrigerated for several hours, but remove it 30 minutes before serving so that it comes to room temperature.

INTERMEDIATE

COFFEE PRALINE CAKE

Photograph, Page 61
Spice Cake filled and frosted with Coffee Buttercream and decorated with Almond Praline. Serves 12 to 14

Cutting an undecorated cake into an unusual shape is one of the quickest ways to produce a striking design. Here a square cake has been cut diagonally, filled, and stacked to produce its triangular shape. Large pieces of almond praline, set around the base and top of the sides, emphasize the strong lines of the cake.

EQUIPMENT

One 9-inch square pan
Baking sheet or marble slab for praline

WORK PLAN

Up to 1 day ahead—
Bake the Spice Cake, and prepare the Almond Praline and Coffee Buttercream.
Baking & Preparation—
About 1¼ hours
Assembly & Decoration—
About 1 hour, including chilling time

RICH PISTACHIO CAKE
·
Recipe, Page 58

COFFEE PRALINE CAKE
.
Recipe, Page 59

RECITE

1 recipe Spice Cake, Page 24

1 recipe Almond Praline, Page 34

1 recipe Coffee Buttercream, Page 28

PREPARATION

1. Bake the cake in a 9-inch square pan. Prepare the almond praline, and when it is cold and hard, break it roughly into jagged, irregular pieces. Prepare the buttercream.

ASSEMBLY & DECORATION

2. When the cake is cool, place it on a flat surface and, with a serrated knife, cut it in half diagonally to form two triangle-shaped layers. Place one layer on a flat serving plate. Spread ¾ to 1 cup of buttercream over the layer with a metal spatula. Top with the second layer. Smooth any buttercream that may have seeped out; refrigerate the cake until the filling sets—15 to 20 minutes.

3. Frost the cake with half the remaining buttercream, beginning with the sides and ending with the top. (For detailed frosting instructions, see page 13.) Refrigerate the cake again for 15 to 20 minutes.

4. Frost the cake a second time and refrigerate the cake for 10 minutes.

5. To decorate the cake, press pieces of praline along the two shorter sides just below the top edge of the cake. The praline should extend above the top. Press the remaining praline along the lower edge of the long side, and set one or two pieces in front of the cake to give the effect of "running off."

STORING & SERVING

Refrigerate the cake until 30 minutes before serving. To serve the cake, make a cut parallel to the base edge, about 5 inches from the tip. Cut this smaller triangle in wedges to the tip. Cut the remaining cake into slices.

ISLAND COCONUT CAKE

Photograph, Page 64
Coconut Genoise filled with Coconut Buttercream and papaya preserves, frosted with Coconut Buttercream, and decorated with toasted coconut. Serves 8 to 10

For the graphically inclined we have created this Mondrian-style design to decorate an old-fashioned coconut cake. To get its golden color, the coconut was spread on a baking sheet and briefly toasted in the oven. After the rules were piped, it was sprinkled with the darker shreds on one side, becoming paler as the design fades across the cake. We used unsweetened coconut, available in health food stores and at some supermarkets, but you can substitute freshly grated coconut.

Inside, a coconut buttercream is combined with papaya preserves, but mango or apricot preserves would be equally good.

EQUIPMENT

Two 8-inch round pans
Ateco #5 round tip
Pastry bag
Baking sheet

WORK PLAN

Up to 1 day ahead—
Bake the Coconut Genoise and prepare the Coconut Buttercream.
Baking & Preparation—
About 1¼ hours
Assembly & Decoration—
About 1¼ hours, including chilling time

RECIPE

1 recipe Coconut Genoise, Page 21

1 recipe Coconut Buttercream, Page 28

½ cup papaya preserves

¼ cup unsweetened grated coconut

PREPARATION

1. Bake the genoise in two 8-inch round pans. Prepare the buttercream.

ASSEMBLY & DECORATION

2. When the genoise is cool, slice each layer in half horizontally with a long serrated knife, to make four layers altogether. Place one layer on a flat serving plate or cardboard round. With a metal spatula, spread ½ cup of buttercream over the cake. Spread one-third of the preserves over the buttercream and top with the second layer. Spread this layer with buttercream and preserves and top with the third layer. Add buttercream and preserves and top with the fourth layer. Smooth any buttercream that may have seeped out, and refrigerate the cake until the filling is firm—15 to 30 minutes.

3. Frost the cake with half the remaining buttercream, beginning with the sides and ending with the top. Refrigerate the cake again for 15 to 20 minutes.

4. Frost the cake a second time, reserving about ½ cup of buttercream for piping. Refrigerate again for 15 to 20 minutes. While the cake is chilling, preheat the oven to 350° to toast the coconut.

5. Spoon buttercream into a pastry bag and attach a #5 tip. With a toothpick, lightly trace the geometric design on the top and sides of the cake. Pipe straight lines of buttercream over the pattern.

6. Spread the coconut on an ungreased baking sheet and toast in the preheated oven for 8 to 10 minutes, until it is lightly browned. Carefully sprinkle the coconut within the design and lightly press into place. Use a toothpick to spread the coconut to meet the buttercream lines. For the side, hold the coconut in the cupped palm of your hand and gently press it against the cake.

STORING & SERVING

The cake may be refrigerated for up to 4 hours, but should sit at room temperature for 30 minutes before serving.

CORAL CAMPARI CAKE

Photograph, Page 65
Genoise sprinkled with Campari, brushed with Crème Anglaise, filled and topped with grapefruit sections, garnished with Crème Anglaise and candied grapefruit peel. Serves 8 to 10.

The genoise, grapefruit and peel, and Crème Anglaise can all be prepared in advance for this glamorous cake. But because Crème Anglaise is fairly thin, the cake should be assembled shortly before serving; otherwise the genoise will become soggy.

EQUIPMENT

Two 8-inch round pans
Small heavy-bottom saucepan
Wire rack

WORK PLAN

Up to 1 day ahead—
Bake the Genoise, and prepare the Crème Anglaise, candied grapefruit peel, and Campari-flavored grapefruit sections.
Baking & Preparation—
About 1½ hours
Assembly & Decoration—
About ½ hour

RECIPE

1 recipe Genoise, Page 20

1 recipe Crème Anglaise, Page 32

4 large pink grapefruits

3¾ cups Campari

¾ cup sugar

PREPARATION

1. Bake the genoise in two 8-inch round pans.

2. Prepare the Crème Anglaise.

3. For the candied peel, use a sharp knife to cut the peel from half of one grapefruit. Scrape the

ISLAND COCONUT CAKE
·
Recipe, Page 62

PRETTY CAKES

CORAL CAMPARI CAKE
·
Recipe, Page 63

bitter white pith from the inside of the rind. Cut the peel into narrow, long strips.

4. Blanch the peel several times to remove its bitterness. In a small heavy bottom saucepan, bring 1½ cups of water and the peel to a boil. Drain the peel and add another 1½ cups of water to the pan. Bring to a boil, drain, and repeat for a total of three times. Drain the peel.

5. In the same saucepan, bring 1 cup of Campari and ½ cup of sugar to a boil. Boil for 1 minute to dissolve the sugar. Add the drained peel and boil until the peel is deep pink—2 to 3 minutes. Drain the candied peel on a wire rack.

6. Cut the peel from the grapefruit, removing as little flesh as possible. Separate the grapefruit into segments. Place the segments in a large, non-aluminum bowl.

7. In a heavy-bottom 1-quart saucepan, mix together 2½ cups of Campari and ¼ cup sugar. Bring to a boil, immediately remove from the heat, and pour over the grapefruit sections. Allow the fruit to soak in the syrup at least until cool, or as long as overnight, to absorb its color and flavor.

ASSEMBLY & DECORATION

8. With a long serrated knife, slice each genoise layer horizontally in half so that you have four layers altogether. Place one layer in a rimmed dish or plate. Sprinkle with a little Campari and brush with Crème Anglaise. Add a second layer and brush with Crème Anglaise. Cover the second layer with grapefruit sections. Top with the third. Sprinkle this layer with Campari and brush with Crème Anglaise. Top with the fourth layer and brush with Crème Anglaise.

9. Decorate the top of the cake with grapefruit sections, still glistening with syrup. Working back to front, arrange the sections with their curved, outer sides facing up, gradually building them up so that they are resting against each other.

10. Spoon the remaining Crème Anglaise around the base of the cake. Set the candied peel slightly off to the side of the front of the cake.

STORING & SERVING

Do not refrigerate the cake, and serve it within the hour.

INTERMEDIATE

OUR FAVORITE CHOCOLATE CAKE

Photograph, Page 68
Chocolate Genoise sprinkled with cognac, rum, or Kahlua, filled with Butter Ganache and crushed Hazelnut Praline, frosted with Butter Ganache, and decorated with chocolate leaves, curls, and Hazelnut Praline. Serves 6 to 8

An abstract ornament of chocolate curls and praline decorates this simple oblong of chocolate cake, and a touch of realism is added with chocolate leaves.

Chocolate can be a highly temperamental ingredient to work with but curls and leaves are fairly easy to make into irresistible decorations. The chocolate for the leaves and curls does not have to be tempered, although if it is not, they should be refrigerated until serving. To make the curls, the chocolate is spread evenly over a flat, unwarped baking sheet and scraped up into curls with a metal pastry scraper. The shape of the curls is determined by the angle of the scraper.

Chocolate leaves may be made using a variety of leaves as molds—lemon, rose, oak, lilac, for example. Use only perfect leaves and wash and dry them beforehand. A few chocolate leaves may break, melt, or not turn out properly when you peel the leaf off the chocolate, so always make more than you need.

EQUIPMENT

Two 8-inch round pans
Small paintbrush (optional)
Twelve fresh lemon or rose leaves

Two heavy baking sheets
Pastry scraper

WORK PLAN

Up to 1 day ahead—
Bake the Chocolate Genoise, and prepare the Hazelnut Praline, Butter Ganache, and chocolate leaves and curls.
Baking & Preparation—
About 3 hours
Assembly & Decoration—
About 1¼ hours

RECIPE

1 recipe Chocolate Genoise, Page 21

1 recipe Butter Ganache, Page 30

½ recipe Hazelnut Praline, Page 34

10 ounces semisweet chocolate

¼ cup cognac, rum, or Kahlua

PREPARATION

1. Bake the genoise in two 8-inch round pans.

2. Prepare the ganache and hazelnut praline. When the praline is cool, grind three-quarters of it in the food processor until it is very finely chopped, being careful not to overgrind. Break the remaining praline into large pieces for decoration. Do not refrigerate the praline, as it will become sticky.

3. Prepare the chocolate leaves and curls. Melt the chocolate in a heatproof bowl over barely simmering water or use a double boiler.

ASSEMBLY & DECORATION

4. When the cake is cool, mark a 6- by 4-inch rectangle on each layer with a toothpick. With a serrated knife, cut the layers to size. Using a long serrated knife, slice each layer in half horizontally to make four layers altogether.

5. Place one layer on a flat serving plate or cardboard round. Sprinkle it with one-third of the liqueur. With a metal spatula, spread the layer with about ½ cup of ganache, then sprinkle with one tablespoon of ground praline. Repeat the pro-

cess with the second and third layers. Top with the fourth layer. Smooth any ganache that has seeped out of the sides of the cake, and refrigerate it until the filling is set, 15 to 20 minutes.

6. Frost the cake with half the remaining ganache, beginning with the sides and ending with the top. Refrigerate the cake again for 15 to 20 minutes.

7. Frost the cake a second time, and refrigerate it until 30 minutes before you are ready to decorate.

8. To decorate the cake, set three large chocolate curls on top of the cake at one corner, gently pressing them into the frosting. (You may need a bit of melted chocolate to help anchor the curls.) Add more curls, gradually building up to form a large cluster. Carefully slip chocolate leaves and shards of praline under and between the curls for balance, extending the arrangement across the top of the cake. At the far corner of the cake, add more praline, leaves, and curls in a smaller cluster.

Making Chocolate Leaves & Curls

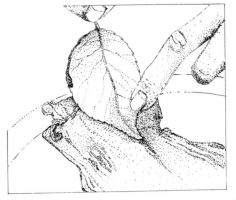

Dip either side of each leaf (the underside to duplicate the pattern of the veins) in chocolate. Cover only one side of the leaf. Alternatively, the chocolate can be brushed on the leaves with a small paintbrush. Refrigerate the leaves on the baking sheet, chocolate-side up, until set— about 20 minutes.

OUR FAVORITE CHOCOLATE CAKE
·
Recipe, Page 66

COFFEE CREME BRULEE
·
Recipe, Page 70

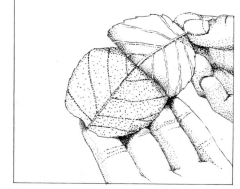

Carefully peel away the leaf, working quickly so that the chocolate does not melt. Refrigerate the chocolate leaves until ready to use.

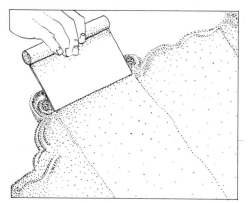

Stir the remaining chocolate until smooth. Using a pastry scraper, evenly spread the chocolate on a baking sheet to a 1/16 to 1/8 inch thickness. Do not overwork the chocolate by spreading it back and forth too many times. Refrigerate the chocolate until set—20 minutes.

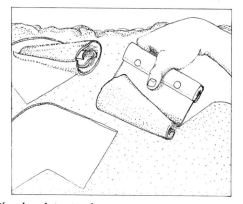

Let the chocolate stand at room temperature for a minute or two (the chocolate will splinter if it is too cold). Using a pastry scraper or the side of a metal spatula, scrape the chocolate into curls. The shape and size of the curls may be varied by the angle of the scraper. If the chocolate becomes too warm, refrigerate it again before continuing. Refrigerate the curls until ready for use.

STORING & SERVING

Refrigerate the cake for several hours, but allow 30 minutes for it to return to room temperature before serving.

ADVANCED

COFFEE CREME BRULEE

Photograph, Page 69
Almond Genoise sprinkled with rum, filled with Coffee Pastry Cream, frosted with Butter Ganache and caramelized Praline, and decorated with sliced almonds. Serves 6 to 8

To get its golden shine, this almond genoise is given a highly unorthodox treatment. The top cake layer is sprinkled with ground praline and put under the broiler so that the praline caramelizes. Obviously, this has to be done carefully. The oven door should be open and the cake watched closely; it may caramelize in less than a minute.

EQUIPMENT

Two 8-inch round pans
Parchment paper
Baking sheet

WORK PLAN

Up to 1 day ahead—
Bake the Almond Genoise, and prepare the Coffee Pastry Cream, Praline, and Butter Ganache.
Baking & Preparation—
About 1½ hours
Assembly & Decoration—
About 1 hour

RECIPE

1 recipe Almond Genoise, Page 21

½ recipe Coffee Pastry Cream, Page 31

½ recipe Praline, omitting the nuts, Page 34

½ recipe Butter Ganache, Page 30

2 tablespoons light rum

2 tablespoons sliced almonds

PREPARATION

1. Bake the genoise in two 8-inch round layers. Prepare the pastry cream, praline, and ganache. Grind the praline in a food processor fitted with a metal blade.

2. Cut an 8-inch oval template from parchment paper.

ASSEMBLY & DECORATION

3. When the genoise has cooled, mark each layer with a toothpick, using the template as a guide. Trim the layers into ovals. Using a long serrated knife, slice each layer in half horizontally to make four layers and set one layer aside.

4. Place one layer on a flat serving plate or cardboard round. Sprinkle the cake with ½ tablespoon of rum and spread with one-third of the pastry cream. Repeat with the second and third layers. Smooth any cream that may have seeped out the sides, and refrigerate the cake until the filling has set—15 to 30 minutes.

5. When the filling is firm, frost the sides of the cake with half the ganache, using a metal spatula. Do not frost the top. Refrigerate until the ganache is firm, 15 to 20 minutes.

6. Frost the sides of the cake a second time, using the remaining ganache. Refrigerate the cake until the top layer is ready to be prepared.

7. Preheat the broiler. Set the remaining genoise layer on an ungreased baking sheet and sprinkle with ground praline. Caramelize the praline.

8. Immediately set the caramelized layer on top of the cake, using a metal spatula to position it. Decorate it with a generous border of sliced almonds, randomly arranged around the edge of the cake where the ganache meets the caramel. The caramel will drip down the sides of the cake, blending with the ganache. Place a few almonds down the sides of the cake as if falling from the border.

Caramelizing Praline

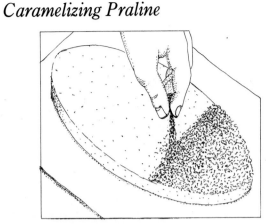

Sprinkle one-third of the ground praline evenly over the top layer. Place under the broiler just until the praline caramelizes, watching the praline closely. Sprinkle half the remaining praline over the caramel and broil again. Repeat a third time if necessary.

STORING & SERVING

The cake can be refrigerated for several hours, and should be served at room temperature.

ADVANCED

CHOCOLATE CAKE WITH WINTER ROSES

Photograph, Page 72
Dense Chocolate Cake frosted with Ganache, and decorated with Ganache, marzipan roses, and Buttercream.
Serves 12 to 14

This dense, moist chocolate cake covered with dark ganache is an ideal canvas for white marzipan roses.

Marzipan roses are not piped; instead they are formed by hand. The marzipan is rolled out quite thinly; and the petals are cut individually with a petal cutter or decorating tube, then shaped, and attached to a center cone of marzipan. To prevent drying out, keep the marzipan covered when you are not working with it.

The white wisps and dots that complete the design are buttercream piped with a small, easy to control, parchment paper cone. Because they require such a small quantity of buttercream, do not feel compelled to make them. The cake is equally lovely without these flourishes.

CHOCOLATE CAKE WITH WINTER ROSES

Recipe, Page 71

EQUIPMENT

One 10-inch springform pan
Rolling pin
Petal cutter or large decorating tip
Parchment paper
Ateco #3 and 6 round, #66 and 69 leaf tips
Pastry bag
Parchment cone

WORK PLAN

Up to 2 days ahead—
Make the marzipan roses and bake the Dense Chocolate Cake.
Up to 1 day ahead—
Prepare the Ganache and Buttercream.
Baking & Preparation—
About 1½ hours
Assembly & Decoration—
About 1½ hours, including chilling time

RECIPE

7 ounces marzipan

1 cup confectioners' sugar or cornstarch

1½ recipes Dense Chocolate Cake, Page 26

1 recipe Ganache, Page 29

4 to 5 tablespoons Buttercream, Page 27

PREPARATION

1. At least 12 hours ahead, make 3 marzipan roses. Sprinkle a work surface with confectioners' sugar or cornstarch. Roll one-quarter of the marzipan into three balls. Shape each ball into an elongated cone. Roll out the remaining marzipan as thinly as possible, sprinkling it and the rolling pin with sugar or cornstarch to prevent sticking and tearing. Cut twenty-eight to thirty petals with a petal cutter. To produce the characteristic wavy edges on the petals, lightly pinch three-quarters of the way around the edge of the circles with your fingers.

2. To form the center of the rose, set a cone on confectioners' sugar or cornstarch and pinch the top third slightly. Very lightly dampen the unpressed, base edge of the petal with cold water, or by dabbing the petal with a damp sponge, and attach the base of the petal to the upper third of the cone. Wrap the petal around the cone, pressing in gently around the top of the petal and extending it above the cone. Before attaching each outer petal, hold it in your palm and press the thicker end with your thumb to cup it slightly. Attach a row of petals to the cone, dampening the edge of the petal first and overlapping them slightly. Beneath this row attach an outer row of petals, center over the inner ones, beginning where the last petal on the second row ended. For authenticity, flute the petals slightly, turning the cone on the sugar or cornstarch. Snip off the rose with a paring knife or scissors and allow to dry on parchment paper.

3. Bake the cake in a 10-inch springform pan. Increase the baking time by about 5 minutes and be sure to test for doneness.

4. Prepare the ganache and buttercream.

ASSEMBLY & DECORATION

5. When the cake is cool, place it on a flat serving plate or cardboard round. Set aside one cup of ganache for the leaves and border. With a metal spatula, frost the cake with half the ganache, beginning with the sides and ending with the top. Refrigerate the cake for 15 to 20 minutes.

6. Frost the cake again with ganache and refrigerate until ready to decorate.

7. Fill a small parchment cone with buttercream. Cut the tip of the cone to make a very small opening. Starting at the center of the cake, make seven wispy streaks radiating out toward the sides. Hold the cone close to the frosting and move the cone in an arc.

8. To pipe the ganache border, lightly trace a wavy line centered about 1 inch from the edge of the cake, using a toothpick. Trace the stems for the grape clusters. Pipe the border, using a #6 tip for the outline and stems, and #3 tip for the grape clusters and tendrils.

9. Attach a #66 tip to the bag and add more ganache if necessary. Pipe leaves at the top of each grape cluster and at the base of the stems. Reserve the bag for the center leaves.

10. Pipe groupings of tiny white dots along the outer sides of the border. Refrigerate the cake for 5 to 10 minutes to chill the ganache.

11. Remove the cake from the refrigerator while the ganache is still slightly soft, or allow it to sit at room temperature for several minutes. Using a small metal spatula or butter knife, carefully position the marzipan roses in the center of the cake. Press them gently into the ganache. Fit the pastry bag with a #69 tip and pipe leaves around and between the roses, arcing the bag slightly to echo the white wisps.

Making Marzipan Roses

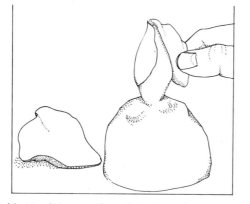

Divide ¼ of the marzipan into 3 equal portions. Roll each piece out into a ball and shape the top into a cone. Roll out the remaining marzipan as thinly as possible and cut about 28 to 30 petals.

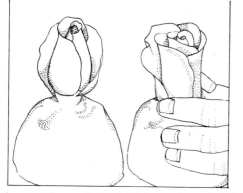

Continue adding moistened petals, each overlapping, and wrap around cone, fluting the edges of the petals to resemble a natural rose. Use a paring knife or scissors to snip off rose. Let dry on parchment paper.

Piping a Grapevine Border

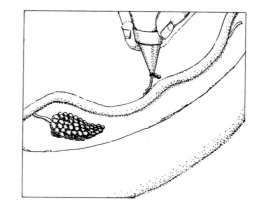

With a #3 tip, pipe clusters of dots to form the bunches of grapes, piping over the wider, top rows of dots to give the bunches height. At random intervals on the border, pipe the tendrils, moving the bag with a spiral motion.

STORING & SERVING

The marzipan roses should not be refrigerated, but the cake can be kept in a cool room for several hours. As this cake is very rich, it should be cut into thin slices.

CRYSTAL LEMON CAKE

Photograph, Page 76
Lemon Layer Cake filled with Swiss Meringue Butter-cream and fig puree, frosted with Buttercream, covered with marzipan, candied violets, and sugar syrup, and decorated with sugar snow. Serves 12 to 14

Sheathed in hard, clear sugar syrup, this marzipan-draped lemon cake seems to be covered with sparkling ice—an effect enhanced by mounds of freshly fallen "snow," granulated sugar mixed with drops of egg white, which surround the cake. A thin layer of buttercream acts as a glue for the marzipan covering and should be thick enough only to make the cake slightly tacky. Once the cake has been covered, it can sit at room temperature for up to two days, but it should not be refrigerated or the marzipan will dry and crack. The sugar snow can be made a week in advance and stored in an airtight container in a cool, dry place (not in the refrigerator).

The final coat of sugar syrup should be poured over the cake no more than two hours before serving. The syrup should be almost clear to light gold when it is melted; if darker, it should be discarded.

EQUIPMENT

One 10-inch round pan, 2-inches deep
Cardboard round
Rolling pin
Candy or frying thermometer
Baking sheet
Wire rack

WORK PLAN

Up to 2 days ahead—
Bake the Lemon Layer Cake, prepare the
Buttercream, fill and cover the cake with marzipan, and prepare the sugar snow.
Up to 2 hours before serving—
Prepare the syrup and glaze cake.
Baking & Preparation—
About 1½ hours
Assembly & Decoration—
About 1 hour

RECIPE

1 recipe Lemon Layer Cake, Page 22

½ recipe Swiss Meringue Buttercream, Page 27

1½ cups coarsely chopped dried figs

¼ cup calvados or Poire William

1 tablespoon honey

14 ounces marzipan

½ cup confectioners' sugar or cornstarch

2 to 3 ounces candied violets

4½ cups granulated sugar

1 to 2 teaspoons egg white

½ cup plus 1 tablespoon corn syrup

½ cup water

PREPARATION

1. Bake the cake in a 10-inch round pan.

2. Prepare the buttercream. Macerate the figs in the liqueur and honey for at least 45 minutes. Puree the mixture in a food processor or blender.

ASSEMBLY & DECORATION

3. When the cake is cool, slice it in half horizontally with a long serrated knife. Place one layer on a cardboard round and spread with the pureed figs, using a metal spatula. Place the second layer on top and with a serrated knife, trim the top edge of the cake to make a beveled edge.

4. Spread a thin coating of buttercream on the sides and top of the cake. (Do not refrigerate.)

5. Roll out the marzipan. Coat hands with cornstarch and confectioners' sugar and drape the cake.

6. With the dull side of a butter knife, make riverlike impressions in the marzipan. Gently press the candied violets into the marzipan over the top and sides of the cake.

7. To make the sugar snow, put 2½ cups of granulated sugar in the large bowl of an electric

CRYSTAL LEMON CAKE
·
Recipe, Page 75

mixer fitted with a paddle attachment if you have one. Add 1 teaspoon of egg white and beat at medium speed until the sugar begins to look damp, about 5 minutes. If it doesn't seem wet enough, add another drop or two of egg white. Spread the sugar on a baking sheet to dry and clump slightly.

8. One or two hours before serving the cake, prepare the sugar syrup. Place the cake on a wire rack set over a shallow pan that has been lined with foil. Bring 2 cups of granulated sugar, ½ cup and 1 tablespoon corn syrup, and ½ cup water to boil in a large, heavy-bottom saucepan over medium-high heat. Stir to combine the ingredients and set a thermometer in the mixture. As soon as the syrup reaches a temperature of 320° to 325°F, quickly take the pan from the heat and pour the syrup on the center of the cake. Let the hot syrup run over the top and down the sides of the cake to cover it completely. Use a metal spatula to smooth the syrup over any unglazed areas. Allow the syrup to harden at room temperature, about 5 minutes.

9. Transfer the cake to a serving plate and surround it with mounds of sugar snow.

Covering a Cake with Marzipan

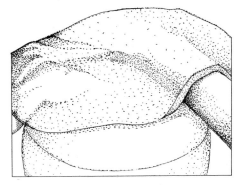

Dust your hands with confectioners' sugar or cornstarch and slide them, palms down, under the marzipan.

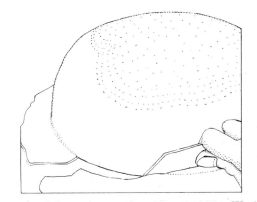

Center and drape the marzipan over the cake. Working with your fingers dusted with confectioners' sugar, smooth the pleats on the sides of the cake. Trim the excess marzipan from the base with a paring knife.

STORING & SERVING

Serve immediately, or within 2 hours. Cut the cake by gently guiding a sharp knife through the glaze, cracking it as you cut.

CHAPTER FIVE

■

Birthday Cakes

TROMPE L'OEIL SLICE
Recipe, Page 82

CANDLELIT CASSIS CAKE
·
Recipe, Page 83

TROMPE L'OEIL SLICE

Photograph, Page 80
Yellow Layer Cake filled and frosted with Ganache.
Serves 8 to 10

This oversize cake "slice" is a simple yellow layer cake filled and frosted with a rich chocolate ganache and trimmed to a wedge shape—a witty, inviting idea sure to be a success with any age. The appearance of the thickly swirled frosting is achieved by making small, circular motions with the spatula when applying the ganache, while the outside rim of filling is piped to complete the effect.

EQUIPMENT

Two 8-inch springform pans
Parchment paper
Ateco #5 round tip
Pastry bag

WORK PLAN

Up to 1 day ahead—
Bake the Yellow Layer Cake and prepare the Ganache.
Baking & Preparation—
About 1 hour
Assembly & Decoration—
About 1¼ hours, including chilling time

RECIPE

1½ recipes Yellow Layer Cake, Page 22

1 recipe Ganache, Page 29, at room temperature

PREPARATION

1. Bake the cake in two 8-inch springform pans. Prepare the ganache.

2. To make a template for trimming the cake layers, trace an 8-inch circle on parchment paper. Draw two straight lines starting from the same point on the circle to form a wide "slice." Cut out the template.

ASSEMBLY & DECORATION

3. When the cake has cooled, place the parchment template on one layer and mark its lines with a toothpick. With a serrated knife, carefully trim the layer to form a "slice." Repeat for the second layer. (For more instructions on trimming cake layers, see page 12.)

4. Place one layer on a serving plate or cardboard round. With a metal spatula, spread ¾ cup of ganache over the cake. Align the second layer over the ganache. Refrigerate until the filling is firm, 15 to 30 minutes.

5. With a small metal spatula, frost the curved back of the cake and then the top, using a little less than half the remaining ganache. Do not frost the flat sides. If some ganache should get on the sides of the cake, remove it with a clean knife or toothpick. Chill the cake for 15 to 20 minutes.

6. Reserve about ¼ cup of ganache. Frost the cake a second time with the remaining ganache, making circular motions with the spatula to achieve a swirled look. Pipe over the filling, using a #5 tip.

Piping a Filling

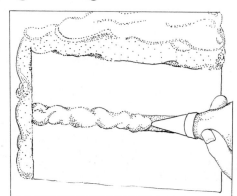

Spoon the reserved ganache into a pastry bag fitted with a #5 tip. Pipe frosting along the outside "filling" on the sides of the cake.

STORING & SERVING

The cake may be covered and refrigerated for up to 8 hours. It should be allowed to sit at room temperature for 30 minutes before serving.

CANDLELIT CASSIS CAKE

Photograph, Page 81
Poppyseed Genoise sprinkled with Crème de Cassis, filled
with black currant preserves and Cassis Buttercream,
frosted with Cassis Buttercream, and decorated
with candles. Serves 8 to 10

Candles are a part of birthday celebrations for all ages, so we designed this black currant-flavored buttercream candle cake that can be decorated by almost any age. Large enough to take any number of real candles, the cake is decorated with a simple pattern of piped buttercream candles.

EQUIPMENT

One 11½- by 15½-inch jelly roll pan
Ateco #84 square tip
Pastry bag
Assorted candles

WORK PLAN

Up to 1 day ahead—
Bake the Poppy Genoise and prepare the Cassis Buttercream.
Baking & Preparation—
About 1¼ hours
Assembly & Decoration—
About 2 hours, including chilling time

RECIPE

1 recipe Poppyseed Genoise, Page 21

1 recipe Cassis Buttercream, Page 28

3 tablespoons Crème de Cassis

2 tablespoons black currant preserves

PREPARATION

1. Bake the genoise in a jelly roll pan. Prepare the buttercream.

ASSEMBLY & DECORATION

2. Place the cooled cake on a flat surface. Using a long serrated knife, trim off the edges of the cake and slice it lengthwise into 4 layers of equal width—the assembled cake will be a little less than 3 inches wide.

3. Put the bottom layer on a cardboard rectangle cut to fit or on a flat serving plate. Sprinkle it with a tablespoon of Crème de Cassis and spread with one-third of the black currant preserves. Using a metal spatula, spread the cake with about ½ cup of buttercream. Top with the second layer. Sprinkle with liqueur and spread with another third of the preserves and ½ cup of buttercream. Repeat for the third layer. Top the cake with the fourth layer. Smooth any buttercream that may have seeped out the sides and refrigerate the cake until the filling is firm—15 to 30 minutes.

4. Reserve about ½ cup of buttercream for decoration. Frost the cake with half the remaining buttercream, beginning with the sides and ending with the top. (For detailed frosting instructions, see page 13.) Refrigerate the cake for 20 to 30 minutes.

5. Frost the cake a second time, and refrigerate for 20 to 30 minutes.

6. To decorate the cake, spoon the remaining buttercream into a pastry bag fitted with a #84 tip. Form a border at the top and base of the cake by piping 2-inch lines at the edges, leaving ¼ inch between the lines. Pipe square "dots" in the ¼-inch intervals. Pipe a continuous line up each corner of the cake. Pipe buttercream "candles" diagonally on the top and sides of the cake, adding dots on top of, or beneath them.

STORING & SERVING

The cake may be served at once or refrigerated, loosely wrapped in plastic, for up to 1 day. Allow it to sit at room temperature for 30 minutes. Just before serving, gently press the candles into the cake, varying the shapes and sizes. When lighting the candles, begin with those in the center of the cake and work outward.

CHOCOLATE GALAXY

·

Recipe, Page 86

MIAMI CASUAL CAKE

Recipe, Page 87

CHOCOLATE GALAXY

Photograph, Page 84
Hazelnut Genoise filled and frosted with Coffee Butter-
cream, covered with marzipan and Ganache Glaze,
and decorated with Coffee Buttercream.
Serves 8 to 10

A winning combination of chocolate and coffee is ac-cented deliciously by a thin layer of marzipan beneath the glaze of this domed cake. To produce the dome shape, the cake is baked in a shallow mixing bowl. Baking time must be adjusted so that the center of the cake cooks through, and as always, the best way to determine if the cake is done is to test it with a cake tester, metal skewer, or toothpick.

The cake may be baked, frosted, and covered with marzipan a day ahead of time. Once the marzipan has been added, though, it should not be refrigerated.

EQUIPMENT

One 7-inch stainless steel bowl, 4-cup capacity
Cardboard round
Ateco #3 round tip
Pastry bag
Rolling pin

WORK PLAN

Up to 1 day ahead—
Bake the Hazelnut Genoise and prepare the Coffee Buttercream and Ganache Glaze.
Baking & Preparation—
About 1¾ hours
Assembly & Decoration—
About 2 hours, including chilling time

RECIPE

1 recipe Hazelnut Genoise, Page 21

½ recipe Coffee Buttercream, Page 28

1 recipe Ganache Glaze, Page 30

1 cup confectioners' sugar or cornstarch

14 ounces marzipan

PREPARATION

1. Bake the genoise in a lightly buttered and floured 7-inch stainless steel bowl for about 45 minutes. Check the cake after 25 to 30 minutes; if the edges are beginning to get very dark, cover them with aluminum foil. Let the cake cool in the bowl to slightly warm before turning it out on a wire rack to cool completely.

2. Prepare the buttercream and ganache glaze.

ASSEMBLY & DECORATION

3. When the cake is cool, place it on a flat surface and use a long serrated knife to slice it horizontally into three layers. The top layer will be rounded.

4. Place the bottom layer on a cardboard round and spread with about ½ cup of buttercream. Put the second layer on top, spread it with butter-cream, and top with the third, domed layer. Smooth any buttercream that may have seeped out the sides and refrigerate the cake until the filling is firm—15 to 30 minutes.

5. With a metal spatula, spread ½ cup of butter-cream over the top and sides of the cake. The buttercream will secure the marzipan to the cake, so it is not necessary to cover crumbs or make the frosting smooth. The cake may be refrigerated but should be brought to room temperature be-fore covering with marzipan. Reserve the remain-ing buttercream for decoration.

6. To prepare the marzipan, sprinkle confection-ers' sugar or cornstarch on a flat work surface. Roll the marzipan to a 16-inch circle, about ⅛-inch thick. Drape the marzipan over the cake, follow-ing the instructions on page 77. Smooth the mar-zipan over the domed top and down the sides of the cake, patting it so that it adheres to the buttercream. Trim away the excess marzipan from the base with a paring knife.

7. To glaze the cake, place it on a wire rack over a shallow pan or sheet of parchment paper. Pour the glaze over the center of the cake so that it runs down the cake and covers it completely.

Use a metal spatula to smooth over any areas that are not covered. Refrigerate the cake for 20 minutes to set the glaze.

8. Spoon the remaining buttercream into a pastry bag fitted with a #3 tip. Use a toothpick to trace the name on top of the cake and carefully pipe over with buttercream. Pipe four-dot diamonds in rows over the top and sides of the cake. Begin at the center above and below the name and at the center of the sides of the letters. Then pipe diamonds of dots alongside the corners of the name. Pipe evenly spaced diamonds in rows from these eight diamonds to the base of the cake.

STORING & SERVING

Place the decorated cake on a flat serving plate. If the cake is not to be served immediately, allow it to sit in a cool dry place for up to 3 hours, but do not refrigerate it.

INTERMEDIATE

MIAMI CASUAL CAKE

Photograph, Page 85
Pistachio Nut Cake filled and frosted with pale green
Swiss Meringue Buttercream and decorated with
marzipan shapes. Serves 8 to 10

This cake is tailor-made for the *artiste manqué* in all of us. Pale green buttercream acts as the canvas for a whimsical collection of brightly colored marzipan shapes. These marzipan decorations should be made a day in advance in order to dry properly. But if they are the most time-consuming aspect of making this cake, they are also the most fun. Copy ours or create your own—they can be made by children as young as two or three. When dry, they are fragile, so it's a good idea to make extras in case of breakage. Small fish cutters, such as the one used for the fish on this cake, are made by Ateco.

Filled and frosted, the cake can be refrigerated for several hours. It should be returned to room temperature before adding the marzipan shapes.

EQUIPMENT

Two 10-inch round pans
Baking sheet
Rolling pin
Fish-shaped cutter
Pencil

WORK PLAN

Up to 2 days ahead—
Make the marzipan shapes.
Up to 1 day ahead—
Bake the Nut Cake and prepare the Swiss Meringue Buttercream.
Baking & Preparation—
About 2 hours
Assembly & Decoration—
About 1¼ hours, including chilling time

RECIPE

7 ounces marzipan

Blue, yellow, red, pink, purple, lavender, and green paste food coloring

2 cups confectioners' sugar or cornstarch

1 recipe Nut Cake, Page 24, made with pistachios

1 recipe Swiss Meringue Buttercream, Page 27

1 teaspoon almond extract

½ pint strawberries

PREPARATION

1. One day in advance, make the marzipan shapes. Divide the marzipan into six parts, which will be colored blue, yellow, red, pink, purple, and lavender respectively. Place all but one in a container covered with plastic wrap to prevent drying.

2. Sprinkle a work surface with confectioners' sugar or cornstarch and knead the marzipan with a dab of paste food coloring until it reaches the desired shade—about 30 seconds to 2 minutes. Reserve the green food coloring for the buttercream. (For detailed information about coloring marzipan, see page 15.) Place the colored marzipan in the covered container. Clean the work surface and sprinkle more confectioners' sugar or corn-

starch for each color. Repeat the coloring process for the remaining chunks of marzipan, returning each to the covered container as it is finished.

3. When shaping marzipan, work with one piece at a time. Clean the work surface and dust with sugar or cornstarch. Liberally sprinkle a baking sheet with sugar or cornstarch, and as each piece of marzipan is shaped, place it on the sheet to dry. Make the fish, then gather the scraps, knead briefly, and return the marzipan to the container.

4. To make the flat red and purple triangles and rectangles, roll out the marzipan to ⅛ inch thickness. Trace the cutting lines with a toothpick, using a template or ruler as a guide. Cut out three or four triangles and four or five rectangles with a paring knife. Gather the scraps and knead briefly. Lightly dust your hands with sugar or cornstarch, pinch off small pieces of marzipan, and roll between your palms to make one or two round balls.

5. Still working with one color at a time, make the spirals, curlicues, and snails. Pinch a piece of marzipan about the size of a walnut and roll it between your palms. Do not overroll the marzipan, as it will crumble. Make eight pink spirals, shaping the skinny rolls into tight and loose coils by wrapping them around a pencil.

6. Make four or five yellow snails of different sizes. Roll four small balls of yellow marzipan between dusted palms, pressing in slightly to elongate them.

7. Use the lavender and blue marzipan to make the foldovers. Between dusted palms, roll out 3-inch lengths of marzipan that taper at the ends. Fold each so that one side is longer than the other. Allow all the shapes to dry, uncovered, at room temperature for 12 to 24 hours.

8. Bake the nut cake, using pistachios, in two 10-inch round pans. Prepare the Swiss meringue buttercream and flavor it with almond extract. Beginning with a tiny amount of paste food coloring, gradually tint the buttercream a pale green.

ASSEMBLY & DECORATION

9. Cut the strawberries lengthwise into thick slices.

10. When the cake is cool, set one layer on a cardboard round or flat serving plate. Spread the cake with ½ cup of buttercream, using a metal spatula. Lay the strawberries on the buttercream. Top with the second layer and smooth any frosting that may have seeped out the sides. Refrigerate the cake until the filling is firm—15 to 30 minutes.

11. Frost the cake with half the remaining buttercream, starting with the sides and ending with the top. Refrigerate the cake for 20 to 30 minutes.

12. Frost the cake a second time. Carefully remove the marzipan shapes from the baking sheet, and gently brush each to remove any sugar or cornstarch. Arrange the shapes on the top and sides of the cake, pressing them gently into the buttercream to hold them in place.

Making Marzipan Fish

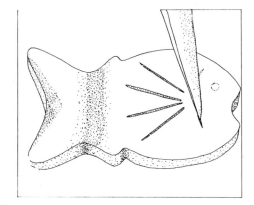

Roll the blue marzipan to ⅛ inch thickness. Using a small fish cutter or parchment template about 1½ inches long and a paring knife, cut out seven or eight fish. With the paring knife, press in the eyes, gills, and fins. Set the fish on the baking sheet, face up, to dry.

STORING & SERVING

The cake may be served immediately or stored in a cool, dry place for up to 3 hours. It should not be refrigerated.

THE CHOCOLATE LOVER'S BIRTHDAY CAKE
·
Recipe, Page 90

THE CHOCOLATE LOVER'S BIRTHDAY CAKE

Photograph, Page 89
Layers of Chocolate Genoise and Chocolate Dacquoise
filled and frosted with White Chocolate Buttercream
and Butter Ganache, decorated with chocolate curls
and Chocolate Dacquoise, and dusted with cocoa.
Serves 18 to 20

Crisp layers of chocolate dacquoise alternate with chocolate genoise to create two textures in this cake. When filled with rich white chocolate buttercream and buttery ganache, and decorated with chocolate curls, it pays very contemporary homage to our love of chocolate.

Conceived especially for great celebrations, this cake can be made in manageable stages: the chocolate curls two days before, the genoise, the dacquoise, buttercream, and ganache one day ahead; and assembled several hours before serving. To achieve the smooth, straight sides of the finished cake, the dacquoise is piped slightly longer than needed. When cool, it is trimmed to match the genoise.

EQUIPMENT

Two baking sheets
Parchment paper
One 11½- by 15½-inch jelly roll pan
Cardboard rectangle
Ateco #6 large round tip
Pastry bag
Fine sieve

WORK PLAN

Up to 2 days ahead—
Make the chocolate curls.
Up to 1 day ahead—
Bake the Chocolate Genoise and Chocolate Dacquoise, and prepare the White Chocolate Buttercream and Butter Ganache.
Baking & Preparation—
About 3½ hours
Assembly & Decoration—
About 1 hour, including chilling time

RECIPE

10 ounces semisweet chocolate

1 recipe Chocolate Genoise, Page 21

2 recipes Chocolate Dacquoise, Page 27

½ recipe White Chocolate Buttercream, Page 28

1 recipe Butter Ganache, Page 30

1 cup cocoa

PREPARATION

1. Make the chocolate curls, following the instructions on page 70. Refrigerate them until ready to decorate the cake.

2. Bake the genoise in a jelly roll pan.

3. Trace 8- by 10-inch rectangles on two sheets of parchment paper. Line two baking sheets with the parchment, tracing-side down. Mix the dacquoise. Pipe the dacquoise rectangles with a large #6 tip. To shape the dacquoise that decorate the sides of the cake, pipe free-form rolls and twig shapes 1½- to 4-inches long in the empty areas on the baking sheets. Bake according to the directions.

4. Prepare the buttercream and ganache.

ASSEMBLY & DECORATION

5. When the genoise has cooled, set it on a flat work surface. Using a long serrated knife, trim off the edge and cut the cake in half to make two 7½- by 10-inch rectangles. Cut a cardboard rectangle to fit the cake.

6. When the dacquoise has cooled, trim both layers to make them the same size as the genoise layers. Holding a layer in the palm of your hand, gently trim away the excess with a paring knife or scissors, making short cuts to prevent crumbling.

7. Anchor one layer of dacquoise on the cardboard with a dab of buttercream. Spread the dacquoise with about ½ cup of ganache using a metal spatula. Place a layer of genoise over the ganache. Spread the genoise with about ½ cup of buttercream. Set the second genoise on the

buttercream and spread with about ½ cup of buttercream. Top with the second dacquoise. Smooth any filling that may have seeped out the sides and refrigerate the cake until the fillings have set, 15 to 30 minutes.

8. Frost the shorter sides of the cake with buttercream. Frost the longer sides with ganache. The sides of the cake are frosted only once, as they will be well covered with chocolate curls and dacquoise rolls. The top of the cake is not frosted.

9. Attach the chocolate curls and dacquoise rolls to the sides of the cake by gently pressing them into the frosting. Arrange them randomly, with some curls extending out from the sides and curls and rolls extending above the sides.

10. To stencil the cake, cut a 5½- by 8-inch rectangle of parchment paper. Put the cake on a serving platter, and slip strips of parchment just under the bottom edges to prevent smudging the plate with cocoa. Center the parchment on top of the cake. With a fine sieve held 4 to 5 inches over the cake, sift the cocoa over the top and sides of the cake. Carefully remove the parchment rectangle and strips.

Piping Dacquoise Rectangles

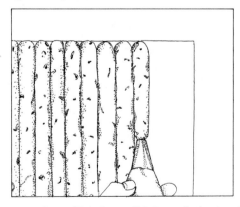

Fit a pastry bag with a large #6 tip and pipe touching lines of dacquoise 10 inches long until you have covered the 8-inch wide area. Use maximum pressure on the bag. Repeat for the second baking sheet.

The cake can be served immediately, or refrigerated for up to 1 hour. Cut this rich cake into small portions using a long, sharp knife.

ADVANCED

AMETHYST BUTTERCREAM BIRTHDAY CAKE

Photograph, Page 92
Orange Genoise sprinkled with Grand Marnier, filled with Chocolate Whipped Cream and Butter Ganache, and frosted and decorated with Swiss Meringue Buttercream. Serves 10 to 12

This traditional, personalized birthday cake is made at once romantic and modern by the colors in the buttercream and piping gel: violet, lavender, pale pink, and green. Writing with tinted piping gel, rather than buttercream, is usually easier for a beginner. (Piping gel, sold at baking supply and specialty stores, is colorless.) The gel squeezes effortlessly from the pastry tip, and since it absorbs food coloring readily, it really stands out against a smooth white frosting. Piping with so many colors is time-consuming, mostly because the pastry bag and tips must be washed and dried thoroughly between each use; this is a good time to use more than one bag.

EQUIPMENT

Two 10-inch round pans
Cardboard round
Turntable
Ateco #1 and #3 round tips
Pastry bags, preferably two or three
Parchment cone

WORK PLAN

Up to 1 day ahead—
Bake the Orange Genoise, and prepare the Butter Ganache and Swiss Meringue Buttercream.
Up to 2 hours ahead—
Prepare the Chocolate Whipped Cream.

AMETHYST BUTTERCREAM BIRTHDAY CAKE

Recipe, Page 91

Baking & Preparation—
About 2 hours
Assembly & Decoration—
About 1½ hours, including chilling time

RECIPE

1 recipe Orange Genoise, Page 21

1½ recipes Swiss Meringue Buttercream, Page 27

1 recipe Chocolate Whipped Cream, Page 29

¼ recipe Butter Ganache, Page 30

3 tablespoons Grand Marnier

Red and violet food coloring (liquid or paste)

3 tablespoons piping gel

Green food coloring (liquid)

Brown food coloring (paste)

PREPARATION

1. Bake the cake in two 10-inch round pans.

2. Prepare the buttercream, whipped cream, and ganache.

ASSEMBLY & DECORATION

3. When the cake has cooled, slice each layer in half horizontally, using a long serrated knife. Place one layer on a cardboard round and sprinkle with 1 tablespoon of Grand Marnier. With a metal spatula, spread the cake with about 1 cup of whipped cream. Position the second layer on top. Sprinkle with 1 tablespoon of Grand Marnier and spread with about ½ cup of ganache. Top with the third layer. Sprinkle the cake with the remaining Grand Marnier and spread with whipped cream. Place the fourth layer on top, smooth any filling that may have seeped out the sides, and refrigerate the cake until the filling is firm, 15 to 30 minutes.

4. Place the cake on a turntable. Reserve about 1 cup of buttercream for decoration. Frost the cake with about half the remaining buttercream, beginning with the sides and ending with the top,

using a metal spatula. Refrigerate the cake for 15 to 20 minutes.

5. Frost the cake a second time with the remaining buttercream, and refrigerate until ready to decorate.

6. Tint the buttercream for decoration, allowing ½ cup for violet, ⅓ cup for lavender, and the remaining tablespoons for pink. To create the lavender, add minute amounts of violet coloring to the buttercream. Add the coloring gradually, mixing well after each addition, to reach the desired shades. Tint the piping gel with green liquid coloring and a bit of brown paste coloring.

7. Return the cake to the turntable. To create the center ring of beads, use a ruler to measure a circle 2 inches from the edge of the cake, lightly marking the buttercream with a toothpick.

8. Partially fill a pastry bag with violet buttercream and attach a #3 tip. Pipe a small bead border over the marks, holding the bag at a 90-degree angle to the cake. Refrigerate the cake for 5 to 10 minutes.

9. Trace and pipe the lettering with a #1 tip.

10. With the toothpick, mark the cake for placement of the flowers. There should be eight evenly spaced nosegays between the bead border and the edge of the cake. Mark seven to eight evenly spaced, centered nosegays on the side of the cake. Pipe the nosegays one color at a time, beginning with the violet centers. The flowers on the side of the cake are smaller than those on top and should be piped with a parchment cone with a ⅛-inch diagonal cut on the tip. Pipe the buttercream in a gentle back-and-forth motion, twisting the bag slightly to give height to the flowers. Pipe the lavender and pink flowers on either side of the violet, making them a bit smaller.

11. Pipe the green gel stems beneath the nosegays, using a #1 tip. Add three stems to the top flowers and two on the sides.

12. Attach the #3 tip to the lavender frosting and pipe a bead border around the top edge of the cake, making the beads slightly larger than those

in the center. With the same tip, pipe the violet border around the base of the cake, making the beads larger than the lavender.

Piping Lettering

Use a toothpick to trace the lettering lightly within the border. Spoon the green gel into a pastry bag fitted with the #1 tip. Holding the bag close to the cake, pipe the gel over the tracing, using light pressure.

STORING & SERVING

The cake may be refrigerated for several hours, but allow it to sit at room temperature for 30 minutes before serving.

ADVANCED

VICTORIAN ROSEBUD CAKE

Photograph, Page 96
Almond Genoise sprinkled with framboise, filled with raspberry jam and Framboise Buttercream, and frosted and decorated with Framboise Buttercream.
Serves 8 to 10

The dusty pink roses that fade from dark to pale and elegant script make this a very sophisticated, feminine birthday cake. To achieve the two-toned roses, a pastry bag is "striped" with two colors of buttercream—a matter of lining the bag first with one color and covering this with the second color.

EQUIPMENT

Two 8-inch round pans
Cardboard round
Turntable
Ateco #2 and #3 round, #68 leaf, and #101 and #104 petal tips
Pastry bags, preferably three or four

WORK PLAN

Up to 1 day ahead—
Bake the Nut Genoise and prepare the Framboise Buttercream.
Baking & Preparation—
About 1½ hours
Assembly & Decoration—
About 2 hours, including chilling time

RECIPE

1 recipe Nut Genoise, Page 21, made with almonds

1½ recipes Framboise Buttercream, Page 28

3 tablespoons framboise

¼ cup raspberry preserves

Red, yellow, green, and brown food coloring

PREPARATION

1. Bake the genoise in two 8-inch round pans. Prepare the buttercream.

ASSEMBLY & DECORATION

2. When the cake has cooled, place one layer on a cardboard round and sprinkle it with half the framboise. Using a metal spatula, spread the cake with raspberry jam and about ½ cup of buttercream. Top with the second layer. Sprinkle the cake with the remaining framboise. Smooth any buttercream that may have seeped out the sides, and refrigerate the cake until the filling is firm—15 to 30 minutes.

3. Set the cake on a turntable. Reserve 2 cups of the buttercream for the decoration. Frost the cake with about half the remaining buttercream, beginning at the sides and ending with the top. Refrigerate the cake again for 20 to 30 minutes.

4. Frost the cake a second time with buttercream and refrigerate until ready to decorate.

5. To begin the decoration, color the 2 cups of buttercream. Tint ½ cup pale pink; ½ cup dusty rose; ½ cup green; ¼ cup dark green; and ¼ cup pale yellow. To achieve the exact shades on the cake, add minute amounts of brown to the pinks and greens. Color 2 tablespoons of the dusty rose to a deeper tone for the lettering.

6. Lightly outline the lettering and flourishes on the top with a toothpick. Stripe a pastry bag with the darkest rose. Pipe the lettering with a #2 tip. Pipe the flourishes along the outline and pipe the small dots over and around the lettering. Finally, pipe two *S*-shaped lines over the center of the bottom flourish. Refrigerate the cake for 15 minutes to set the lettering.

7. With a toothpick, lightly mark the design for the rosebuds, tendrils, leaves, and yellow flowers on the top of the cake. On the side of the cake, mark the pattern of scrolls and rosebuds. If the buttercream frosting begins to soften while the design is being traced, refrigerate the cake for 5 to 10 minutes, then continue.

8. Partially fill a pastry bag with lighter green frosting and fit the bag with a #3 tip. Pipe the green tendrils on top of the cake. With the same tip, pipe the design on the side. Pipe over the scrolls with a back-and-forth motion.

9. Fit a #104 tip into a pastry bag, adjusting the tip so that the wide end is directed to the seam of the bag. Stripe the bag along the creased seam with the darkest rose. Fill over the stripe with pale pink buttercream. Pipe the flowers over the design.

10. Spoon pale pink frosting into a pastry bag and attach a #101 tip. Pipe the tiny rosebuds and dots along the side of the cake, following the tracing.

11. Spoon yellow buttercream into a pastry bag and fit with the #3 tip. Pipe tiny dot flowers on top of the cake.

12. For the leaves, stripe a bag with dark green frosting and fill with the lighter green. Attach a #68 tip, adjusting it so that its center opening is positioned at the darker stripe. Pipe leaves under and around the rosebuds and yellow flowers and along the flourishes.

Striping a Pastry Bag

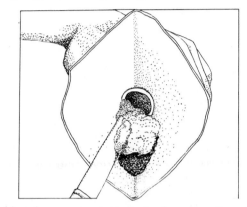

Fold and crease an empty pastry bag along the seam. With a butter knife, carefully fill in the crease with darkest rose buttercream. To prevent smudging, cover the stripe with a thin layer of pink. Add more pink to fill the bag half-full.

Piping Lettering

With a #3 tip, pipe in the outline for lettering, controlling the bag so that the darker shading is always on the same side. Pipe over the H, B, and y's in a light, back-and-forth motion to make the small ridges.

VICTORIAN ROSEBUD CAKE

·

Recipe, Page 94

Piping a Rosebud

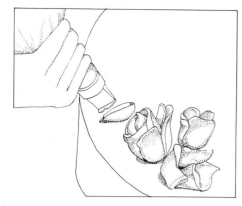

With a #104 or #101 tip and holding the bag so that the darker frosting will be at the base of the flowers, pipe the rosebuds. With medium pressure, pipe the center petal, moving the bag in a tight arc. Pipe the second and third petals on opposite sides, overlapping the petals in the center.

Piping Rosebuds and Scrolls

For the sides of the cake, lightly outline scrolls and rosebuds with a toothpick. Pipe the green scrolls with a #3 tip, piping over their curves with a short back-and-forth motion. Use a #101 tip for the rosebuds and dots.

STORING & SERVING

The cake can be refrigerated for several hours, but should sit at room temperature for 30 minutes before serving.

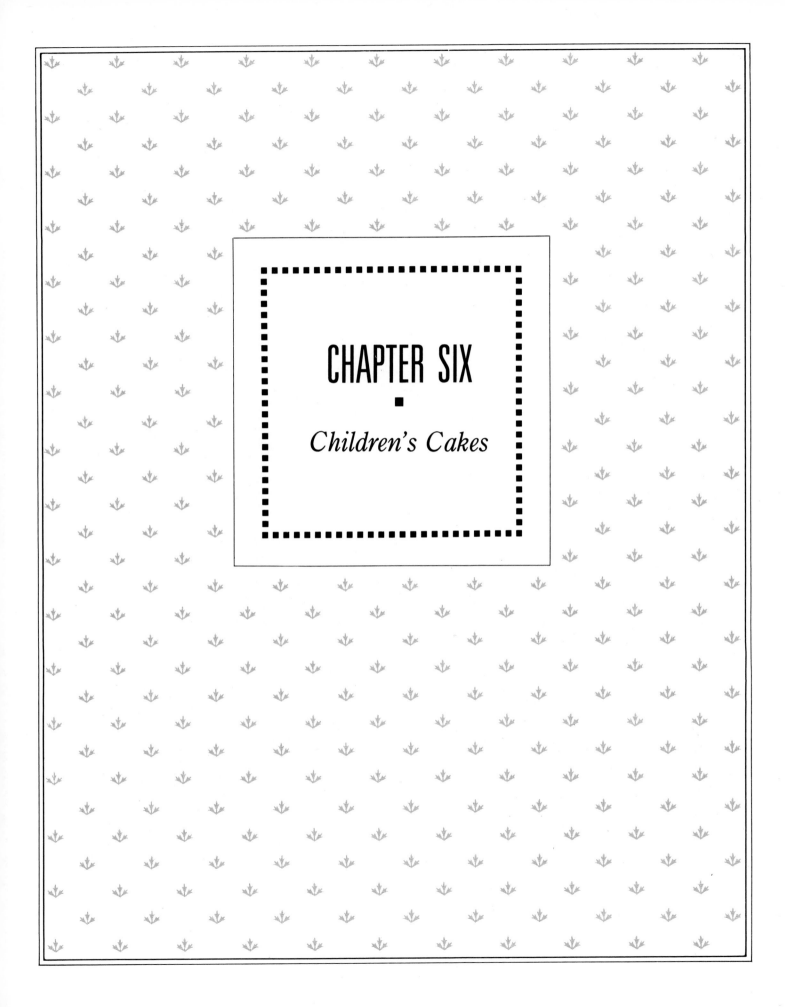

CHAPTER SIX

•

Children's Cakes

SILLY CUPCAKES
·
Recipe, Page 102

PRETTY CAKES

THE GIANT'S CUPCAKE

Recipe, Page 103

SILLY CUPCAKES

Photograph, Page 100
Yellow cupcakes frosted with Confectioners' Sugar
Frosting and decorated with animal crackers piped with
Confectioners' Sugar Frosting. Serves 16 to 20

Children love these colorful cupcakes, each topped with a decorated animal cracker, not least because they can help bake and decorate them. The cupcakes are baked in regular and miniature sizes, and each is spread with a generous swirl of pastel confectioners' sugar frosting. The same frosting is used for piping the manes, fleece, tails, and fur on the "animals." To be sure of getting twenty-four unbroken animal crackers, buy two boxes. Fast to do, these cupcakes can be frosted up to a day ahead, then kept wrapped, and refrigerated, but add the crackers just before serving.

EQUIPMENT

One 12-form standard cupcake pan
One 12-form miniature cupcake pan
Twelve cupcake papers
Twelve petit four cups
Baking sheet
Ateco #8 round tip
Pastry bag

WORK PLAN

Up to 1 day ahead—
Bake the cupcakes, prepare the Confectioners' Sugar Frosting, and frost cupcakes and animal crackers.
Baking & Preparation—
About 1 hour
Assembly & Decoration—
About 45 minutes

RECIPE

1 recipe Yellow Layer Cake, Page 22

1 recipe Confectioners' Sugar Frosting, Page 29

Green, yellow, copper, red, blue liquid food coloring

24 animal crackers

PREPARATION

1. Prepare the cake batter and line the cupcake pans with paper cups. Fill each about three-quarters full and bake in a preheated 350°F oven. Test smaller cupcakes after 7 to 10 minutes; larger ones after 13 to 15. To test for doneness, insert a toothpick into one of the cupcakes in the center of each pan. Cool the cakes slightly in the pans on wire racks, then remove the cakes and allow to cool completely on wire racks.

2. Prepare the frosting. Tint the frosting to make ⅔ cup each of green, yellow, and copper, and ½ cup each pink and blue.

ASSEMBLY & DECORATION

3. When the cupcakes are cool, liberally frost each one with green, yellow, or copper frosting. Refrigerate the cupcakes.

4. Spread the animal crackers, face up, on a baking sheet. Spoon tinted frosting into a pastry bag fitted with a #8 tip. Pipe markings on each cracker—mane and tail for the lion, wool for the sheep, and so on. Use both the pink and blue frosting. Refrigerate the crackers to set the frosting.

5. Decorate the cupcakes by setting one cracker on each, gently pressing it into the frosting.

STORING & SERVING

The frosted cupcakes and crackers can be refrigerated for up to 1 day. Arrange the crackers on the cupcakes up to 1 hour before serving, and allow them to sit at room temperature to soften the frosting.

THE GIANT'S CUPCAKE

Photograph, Page 101
Chocolate Layer Cake filled and frosted with Confectioners' Sugar Frosting and chocolate chips.
Serves 25 to 30

Giant-sized and wrapped in a star-spangled parchment paper cup, this giant cupcake will delight every child at the party. Beneath the confectioners' sugar frosting spiked with ground chocolate chips is a four-layer chocolate cake baked in different sized pans to achieve the cupcake shape.

This larger-than-life cupcake will serve a large party but it can easily be reduced by using smaller pans and making less batter and buttercream. To make a cake half the size, use one recipe for Chocolate Layer Cake, 1½ recipes of frosting, and 6 ounces of semisweet chocolate chips. Bake only three layers in three 6-inch pans and trim two of these to 5 inches and 4 inches round respectively. Assemble the cake so that the 5-inch layer is on the bottom, the 6-inch layer next, and the 4-inch layer on top of the cake. This modified version will serve ten to twelve hungry children easily.

We recommend you use parchment paper to wrap the cake, not colored paper, as the waxy surface of parchment will not absorb the frosting. It can be decorated with stars, or with crayons or fingerpaints before pleating.

EQUIPMENT

One each 6-, 7-, 8-, and 9-inch round pans
Two cardboard rounds
Parchment paper
One package colored stars

WORK PLAN

Up to 1 day ahead—
Bake the Chocolate Layer Cakes and prepare the Confectioners' Sugar Frosting.
Baking & Preparation—
About 2 hours
Assembly & Decoration—
About 1½ hours, including chilling time

RECIPE

2 recipes Chocolate Layer Cake, Page 22

3 recipes Confectioners' Sugar Frosting, Page 29

12 ounces semisweet chocolate chips

PREPARATION

1. Mix the cake batter and fill each cake pan one-third full. Bake as directed.

2. Prepare the frosting. Coarsely grind the chocolate chips in a food processor. Reserve ½ cup for decoration and stir the remainder into the frosting.

ASSEMBLY & DECORATION

3. When the cakes have cooled, place the 7-inch layer on two cardboard rounds that have been taped together. With a metal spatula, spread the cake with a generous ½ cup of frosting. Center the 8-inch layer over the frosting and spread with frosting. Center the 9-inch layer on top and spread with frosting. Smooth any frosting that may have seeped out the sides and refrigerate the cake until the filling has set—about 20 minutes.

4. Mound ¼ cup of frosting in the center of the cake. Using a serrated knife, bevel the top edge of the 6-inch layer, following the instructions on page 12. Position the layer in the center of the cake. Frost the sides of the smaller layer, filling in to create a smooth slope to the 9-inch layer. Refrigerate the cake to chill the frosting—about 20 minutes.

5. With a metal spatula, frost the entire cake, beginning with the sides and ending with the top. (For detailed frosting instructions, see page 13.) Refrigerate the cake again for 20 minutes.

6. Frost the cake a second time, mounding the frosting to create a smooth, rounded top. Sprinkle ground chocolate chips over the top of the cake.

7. Make the parchment cup and wrap it around the cake. Glue the stars to the paper cup.

Making a Parchment Cup

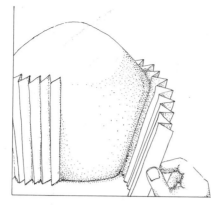

Measure the circumference of the cake at its widest point, and its height at the sides. Cut two rectangular pieces of parchment paper to these measurements. Starting at the short end, pleat each paper like a fan. Tape the pleated papers together at one end and wrap the paper around the cake, overlapping the pleats to fit. Tape the seam and gently press the paper into the frosting to hold it in place.

STORING & SERVING

The filled and frosted cupcake can be refrigerated, loosely wrapped, for up to 1 day. Allow the cake to sit at room temperature 45 minutes before serving.

GREATEST HITS CAKE

Photograph, Page 105
Dense Chocolate Cake frosted with Butter Ganache and decorated with a marzipan disc. Serves 10 to 14

This rich chocolate cake frosted with dark ganache makes a perfect record to give to a teenager. The grooves are made very easily with a triangle-shaped baker's comb, pressing it lightly into the frosting as the cake is rotated on a turntable. In the center of the record is a marzipan "label." This will need to dry several hours or overnight after rolling out and cutting, and because dried marzipan is fragile, you may want to make at least one extra.

EQUIPMENT

Pastry cutter or glass, 4 inches in diameter
One 10-inch springform pan
Rolling pin
Cardboard round
Turntable
Baker's comb
Ateco #1 round tip and pastry bag, or parchment cone

WORK PLAN

Up to 1 day ahead—
Make the marzipan disc, bake the Dense Chocolate Cake, and prepare the Butter Ganache.
Baking & Preparation—
About 1¼ hours
Assembly & Decoration—
About 1 hour, including chilling time

RECIPE

½ cup confectioners' sugar or cornstarch

2 ounces marzipan

1 recipe Dense Chocolate Cake, Page 26

1 recipe Butter Ganache, Page 30

PREPARATION

1. Sprinkle a flat work surface with confectioners' sugar or cornstarch. Roll out the marzipan to a 5-inch circle, about ⅛ inch thick. With a pastry cutter or glass, cut a 4-inch round. Punch a hole in the center of the round with the top of a round pastry tip or an unsharpened pencil. Place the disc on a kitchen towel and allow to dry at room temperature for several hours or overnight.

2. Bake the cake in a 10-inch springform pan. Prepare the ganache.

ASSEMBLY & DECORATION

3. When the cake is cool, place it on a cardboard round. Using a metal spatula, frost the cake with

GREATEST HITS CAKE
·
Recipe, Page 104

half the ganache, beginning with the sides and ending with the top. Refrigerate the cake until the frosting has set—15 to 20 minutes.

4. Reserve ⅓ cup of ganache for the lettering. Frost the cake a second time with the remaining ganache. Comb the frosting, then refrigerate the cake to set the ganache.

5. Pipe the lettering on the marzipan disc with a pastry bag fitted with a #1 tip or a parchment cone with a small opening. Place the disc on a kitchen towel for stability and lightly outline the lettering with a pencil. Pipe ganache over the outline. Allow the lettering to dry.

6. Using a metal spatula or butter knife, center the marzipan disc on the cake.

Using a Baker's Comb

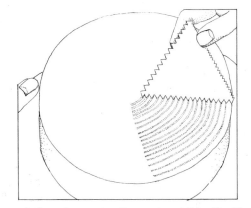

To comb the cake, center it on a turntable. Position the medium-tooth side of the comb along the cake's radius so that its outer edge is level with the outside of the cake. Holding the comb lightly against the frosting, quickly and steadily rotate the turntable until the grooves marked by the comb meet.

STORING & SERVING

The cake may be served immediately or refrigerated for several hours, but it should sit at room temperature for 30 minutes to soften the frosting.

THE ENCHANTED FLOWERPOT

Photograph, Page 108
Chocolate Layer Cake filled and frosted with Chocolate Buttercream, decorated with crushed chocolate wafers and fresh flowers. Serves 18 to 20

A bouquet of fresh flowers adds authenticity to this chocolate flowerpot cake. Four cake layers are filled and frosted with terra-cotta colored chocolate buttercream to form the flowerpot, and crushed chocolate wafers are sprinkled on top to resemble earth. Finally the flowers are inserted in lengths of plastic drinking straws which have been "planted" in the "earth." Because the assembled cake is fairly heavy, it should stand on two cardboard rounds that have been taped together for support.

EQUIPMENT

Three 6-inch round pans
One 7-inch round pan
Parchment paper
Two cardboard rounds
Eight to ten plastic straws

WORK PLAN

Up to 1 day ahead—
Bake the Chocolate Layer Cakes and prepare the Chocolate Buttercream.
Up to 30 minutes ahead—
Decorate with fresh flowers and leaves.
Baking & Preparation—
About 1½ to 2 hours
Assembly & Decoration—
About 1½ hours including chilling time

RECIPE

2 recipes Chocolate Layer Cake, Page 22

2 recipes Chocolate Butttercream, Page 28

Red food coloring

1 cup crushed chocolate wafers

8 to 10 fresh flowers

5 to 6 sprigs fresh leaves

PREPARATION

1. Bake the cakes in three 6-inch and one 7-inch round pans. Prepare the buttercream and add a small amount of red food coloring to achieve a terra-cotta shade.

2. Cut two parchment discs to use as templates, one 5-inches in diameter and another 5½-inches.

ASSEMBLY & DECORATION

3. When the cakes have cooled, set them on a flat surface. Using the parchment templates as guides, trim two 6-inch layers to 5- and 5½-inches respectively.

4. Assemble and fill the cake. Refrigerate until the filling has set—15 to 30 minutes.

5. Frost the cake, then refrigerate to chill the buttercream—about 20 minutes.

6. Frost the cake a second time. Sprinkle the crushed chocolate wafers on top, leaving a ½-inch border for the top lip of the flowerpot.

7. To hold the flowers, cut a 1½-inch length of plastic straw for each. Insert the straws into the cake, then add the flowers. Complete the design with leaves pressed directly into the cake.

Assembling a Flowerpot Cake

Place the 5-inch layer on two cardboard rounds that have been taped together. With a metal spatula, spread ½ cup of buttercream over the cake. Top with the 5½-inch layer and frost with ½ cup of buttercream. Add the 6-inch layer and spread with another ½ cup of buttercream. Center the 7-inch layer on the frosting and spread with ½ cup of buttercream.

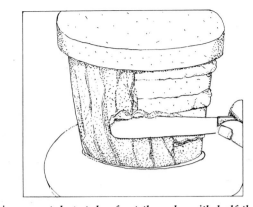

Using a metal spatula, frost the cake with half the remaining buttercream, beginning with the sides and ending with the top. Gradually add extra buttercream to the sides of the three bottom layers to create a smooth line. Run the spatula under the extended edge of the top layer to form the lip of the flowerpot.

STORING & SERVING

Without the flowers, the cake can be refrigerated for up to a day, but should sit at room temperature for 1 hour to soften the frosting. Be sure to remove the straws when the flowers are taken off.

WILD ROSE CAKE

Photograph, Page 109
Lemon Genoise filled with Lemon Pastry Cream and fresh peaches, frosted and decorated with Swiss Meringue Buttercream roses. Serves 6 to 8

Stylized roses tumble over this dome cake, creating the illusion of a lush summer bouquet specially picked for someone's birthday. Buttercream roses take time to make but can be done well in advance. Once frozen, they can be covered with plastic wrap or foil and kept in the freezer for up to a week. When the roses are added to the cake, they should be chilled for at least fifteen minutes before handling.

THE ENCHANTED FLOWERPOT
Recipe, Page 106

P R E T T Y   C A K E S

WILD ROSE CAKE

Recipe, Page 107

EQUIPMENT

One 6-inch diameter ovenproof bowl, 3 cup capacity
Ateco #70 leaf and #104 petal tips
Pastry bag
Flower nail
Waxed paper

WORK PLAN

Up to 1 week ahead—
Prepare the Swiss Meringue Buttercream and pipe the roses.
Up to 1 day ahead—
Bake the Lemon Genoise, and prepare the Lemon Pastry Cream.
Up to 4 hours ahead—
Slice the peaches and assemble the cake.
Baking & Preparation—
About 2½ hours
Assembly & Decoration—
About 1½ hours, including chilling time

RECIPE

1 recipe Swiss Meringue Buttercream, Page 27

Red and green food coloring

½ recipe Lemon Genoise, Page 21

½ recipe Lemon Pastry Cream, Page 31

2 fresh peaches

PREPARATION

1. Prepare the buttercream. With a small amount of red food coloring, tint 3 cups pale pink. Use green food coloring to tint the remaining 1 cup pale green.

2. To pipe the roses, fit a pastry bag with a #104 tip and spoon pink buttercream into the bag. Following the instructions on page 54, pipe about thirty roses of varying sizes. Freeze the roses for 15 minutes or longer. You should have about 1 cup of buttercream left over.

3. Bake the genoise in a lightly buttered and floured 6-inch bowl.

4. Prepare the pastry cream. Peel and thinly slice the peaches.

ASSEMBLY & DECORATION

5. Set the cool cake on a flat surface and, using a long serrated knife, slice it horizontally into three layers. Place the bottom, flat layer on a cardboard round or serving plate. Spread the cake with half the pastry cream. Cover the pastry cream with a layer of sliced peaches. Add the second layer. Spread this with the remaining pastry cream and cover with peaches. Top with the rounded layer. Smooth any filling that may have seeped out the sides, and chill the cake for 15 to 20 minutes to set.

6. Frost the cake with a thin layer of pink buttercream, using a metal spatula. Because the entire cake will be covered with roses, it is not necessary to finish the frosting perfectly.

7. To decorate the cake, chill the roses; the cake should be at room temperature. Using a metal spatula and your fingers, place the roses over the entire surface of the cake. Pipe in the leaves with a #70 tip.

STORING & SERVING

The decorated cake may be refrigerated for several hours but should be allowed to sit at room temperature for about an hour before serving.

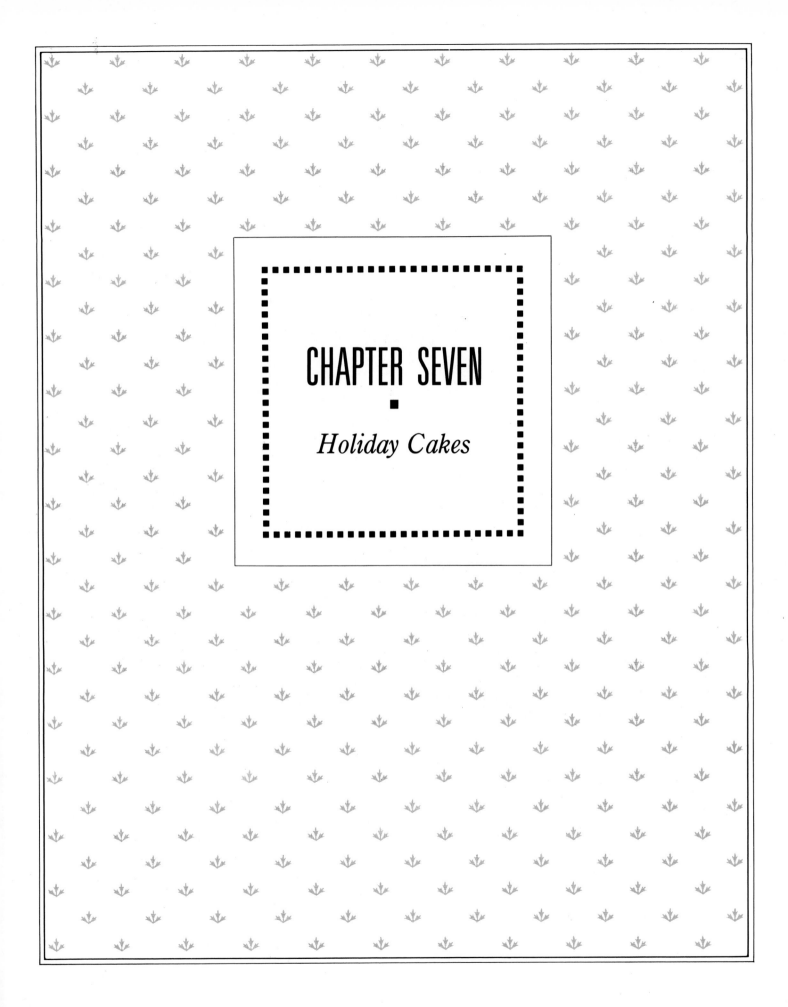

CHAPTER SEVEN

■

Holiday Cakes

STARRY NEW YEAR CAKE

Recipe, Page 113

STARRY NEW YEAR CAKE

Photograph, Page 112
Spice Cake filled and frosted with Amaretto Buttercream,
covered and decorated with marzipan, and sprinkled
with gelatin "glitter." Serves 10 to 12

Colorful marzipan stars make this New Year's celebration cake dazzle. Their vibrant colors come from kneading concentrated paste food colorings into the marzipan, which is then rolled and cut into stars and letters. The marzipan shapes are not dried after rolling and cutting, but are arranged on the cake while they are still moist so that they conform to its shape. A finishing touch is provided by a sprinkling of festive "glitter," made from tiny pieces of bakers' gelatin. Gelatin is available in sheets through bakers' supply shops; see Sources of Supply.

EQUIPMENT

Two 10-inch round pans
Cardboard round
Rolling pin
Letter cutters
Star cutters, 1, 2, and 4 inches from point to point
Pastry brush

WORK PLAN

Up to 1 day ahead—
Bake the Spice Cake and prepare the Amaretto Buttercream. Fill and frost the cake, and decorate with marzipan.
Baking & Preparation—
About 1½ hours
Assembly & Decoration—
About 1 hour

RECIPE

1 recipe Spice Cake, Page 24

½ recipe Amaretto Buttercream, Page 28

28 ounces marzipan

1 cup confectioners' sugar

Red, orange, yellow, green, and turquoise paste food coloring

1 sheet bakers' gelatin

PREPARATION

1. Bake the cake in two 10-inch round pans. (To bake the cake in one layer, choose a pan with 4-inch sides.)

2. Prepare the buttercream.

ASSEMBLY & DECORATION

3. Set one layer on a cardboard round. With a metal spatula, spread the cake with about ½ cup of buttercream. Place the second layer on top and smooth any filling that may have seeped out the sides. Refrigerate the cake to set the filling—15 to 20 minutes.

4. With a serrated knife, bevel the top edge of the cake, following the instructions on page 12. Frost the cake with a thin layer of buttercream, beginning with the sides and ending with the top. The cake may be refrigerated at this point but should be brought to room temperature before adding the marzipan.

5. Roll out half the marzipan to a 16-inch circle. Center and drape the marzipan over the cake, following the illustrated instructions on page 77.

6. Divide the remaining marzipan into six parts. Color two parts red and one each of the remaining parts yellow, orange, green, and turquoise. Working with one part at a time, knead a dab of color into the marzipan until the desired shade is reached—30 seconds to 2 minutes. Add more color gradually, kneading it in completely each time. Keep the remaining marzipan in a covered bowl while working on each piece.

7. To decorate the cake, use a toothpick to lightly indicate the position of the letters on top of the cake. Sprinkle a work surface with confectioners' sugar and roll out the red marzipan to ⅛ inch thickness. Cut out the letters with letter cutters. Brush away any sugar on top of the letters. Brush

the underside of each letter very lightly with cold water and place it in position on the cake, pressing gently to fix it in place.

8. Cut the stars from the remaining marzipan with star-shaped cutters. (We used one large, two medium, and two small stars in each color.) As the stars are cut, brush them lightly with water and place them on the cake.

9. Cut the sheet of gelatin into small pieces with scissors and sprinkle the pieces over the cake.

STORING & SERVING

Transfer the cake to a serving platter. The cake may sit at room temperature for several hours but should not be refrigerated.

SIMPLE

A CHOCOLATE VALENTINE

Photograph, Page 116
Chocolate Layer Cake filled with cherry preserves and Chocolate Buttercream, frosted with Chocolate Buttercream, and decorated with assorted chocolates.
Serves 8 to 10

Designed to steal anyone's heart, this buttercream-filled cake conceals the thinnest coating of cherry preserves which add an intriguing tang to the chocolate layers. The cake may be made in 8-inch heart-shaped pans if you have them, but it works just as well baked in round pans and trimmed into a heart shape.

EQUIPMENT

Two 8-inch round pans
Parchment paper

WORK PLAN

Up to 1 day ahead—
Bake the Chocolate Layer Cake and prepare the Chocolate Buttercream. Fill and frost the cake.
Up to 1 hour ahead—
Decorate the cake with chocolates.
Baking & Preparation—
About 1¼ hours
Assembly & Decoration—
About 1½ hours, including chilling time

RECIPE

1 recipe Chocolate Layer Cake, Page 22

1 recipe Chocolate Buttercream, Page 28

2 tablespoons cherry preserves

½ pound dark and milk chocolates

PREPARATION

1. Bake the cake in two 8-inch round pans. Cut an 8-inch heart-shaped template from parchment paper.

2. Prepare the buttercream.

ASSEMBLY & DECORATION

3. Using the parchment template as a guide, mark the cake layers with a toothpick, as on page 12. Trim each layer into a heart shape, using a serrated knife.

4. Place one layer on a cardboard round or flat serving plate. Using a metal spatula, spread it with the cherry preserves and then with about ½ cup of buttercream. Position the second layer on top and smooth any frosting that may have seeped out the sides. Refrigerate the cake until the filling is firm—15 to 30 minutes.

5. Frost the cake with half the remaining buttercream, beginning with the sides and ending at the top. (For detailed frosting instructions, see page 13.) Refrigerate the cake again for 15 to 20 minutes.

6. Frost the cake a second time with the remaining buttercream. Refrigerate the cake for up to 1 hour before serving.

7. When ready to serve, decorate the top of the cake with a cluster of chocolates, pressing them gently into the buttercream. Arrange more chocolates, some still in their paper cups, at the base of the cake.

STORING & SERVING

Refrigerate the cake, loosely wrapped in plastic, for up to 1 day, but allow it to sit at room temperature for 30 minutes before serving. This cake travels very well but the chocolates should be added just before serving. To serve, cut the cake into thin slices and include 1 or 2 chocolates with each piece.

INTERMEDIATE

MARDI GRAS RUM CAKE

Photograph, Page 117
Pecan Genoise flavored with rum, filled with Praline
Buttercream, frosted with Rum Buttercream, and
decorated with a marzipan mask and confetti.
Serves 8 to 10

In appearance, only the marzipan mask hints at the dark, rich flavors of rum and praline that spike this genoise and make it such an appropriate celebration of the last day before Lent fasting. Colored marzipan shapes in traditional colors of this festival—gold for power, green for faith, and purple for justice—and other bright hues add a carnival atmosphere.

The mask is made by molding tinted marzipan over a traditional Halloween mask; it will need to dry for two days before use (the confetti also needs at least twelve hours to harden). Even then, the mask is quite fragile, so you may want to make an extra.

EQUIPMENT

Halloween mask
Rolling pin
Two 8-inch round pans
½ yard green ribbon, ¼ inch wide

WORK PLAN

Up to 1 week ahead—
Make the marzipan mask.
At least 12 hours ahead—
Make the marzipan confetti, bake the Pecan Genoise, and prepare the buttercreams.
Baking & Preparation—
About 2¼ hours

Assembly & Decoration—
About 1½ hours, including chilling time

RECIPE

14 ounces marzipan

Orange, brown, blue, green, red, and purple paste food coloring

2½ pounds confectioners' sugar or cornstarch

1 recipe Nut Genoise, Page 21, made with pecans

½ recipe Praline Buttercream, Page 28

½ recipe Rum Buttercream, Page 28

¼ cup rum

PREPARATION

1. At least two days ahead, make the marzipan mask. Tint 7 ounces of marzipan gold, using orange food coloring darkened with a little brown. Sprinkle a work surface with confectioners' sugar or cornstarch and knead the tinted marzipan for 30 seconds to 2 minutes to reach the desired color.

2. Roll out the marzipan to a ¼-inch thick oval that is about an inch or two longer and wider than the mask. Liberally dust the inside of the mask with sugar or cornstarch. Slide your hands, palms down, under the marzipan and drape it over the inside of the mask. Gently press the marzipan to the contours of the mask and trim off the surplus. Mound sugar or cornstarch in a large bowl and set the mask on top so that the marzipan is exposed to the air.

3. To support the mask on the cake, roll two 1-inch balls from the scrap marzipan between your palms. Set the balls and mask aside to dry for at least two days.

4. Divide the remaining marzipan into six pieces. Color each gold, blue, green, red, lavender, and purple respectively. To achieve the shades on our cake, add tiny amounts of brown coloring to the red, green, and gold. Work with one piece of marzipan at a time, keeping the others in a covered container.

A CHOCOLATE VALENTINE
·
Recipe, Page 114

MARDI GRAS RUM CAKE
·
Recipe, Page 115

5. Sprinkle a work surface with sugar or cornstarch and roll out each piece to a ¹⁄₁₆ inch thickness. Brush away any sugar or cornstarch on the marzipan. With a paring knife, cut the marzipan into small diamonds ½ to 1 inch long. Spread the diamonds in a single layer on parchment or waxed paper to dry for at least twelve hours.

6. Bake the genoise in two 8-inch round pans. Prepare the buttercreams.

ASSEMBLY & DECORATION

7. When the cake layers have cooled, slice each in half horizontally, using a long serrated knife. Place one layer on a cardboard round or flat serving plate. Sprinkle the layer with 1 tablespoon of rum. Using a metal spatula, spread the cake with about ½ cup of praline buttercream. Position a second layer on top. Sprinkle with rum and spread with buttercream. Continue for the third and fourth layers, sprinkling the top layer with the remaining rum. Smooth any filling that may have seeped out between the layers. Refrigerate the cake for 15 to 30 minutes, until the filling is set.

8. Frost the cake with half the rum buttercream, beginning with the sides and ending with the top. Refrigerate the cake again for 20 to 30 minutes.

9. Frost the cake a second time with the remaining rum buttercream. Refrigerate the cake until 30 minutes before decorating.

10. To finish the mask, carefully lift the marzipan off the Halloween mask and brush off the sugar or cornstarch. Curl the ribbon and thread it through the hole in the mask. Place the marzipan balls on top of the cake as supports, one ball to be under the ribbon hole and the second on the opposite side of the mask. Set the mask on the cake, leaning it against the balls. Gently press the confetti on the top and sides of the cake and sprinkle onto the plate.

Making a Marzipan Mask

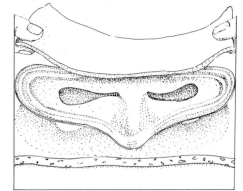

Drape the marzipan over the inside of the mask that has been dusted with confectioners' sugar or cornstarch, gently pressing it to the contours. With a paring knife, trim the edges and cut out the eyes. With the knife, pierce a hole in one corner of the marzipan for the ribbon. Set the mask in a bowl of confectioners' sugar or cornstarch, marzipan-side up, to dry.

STORING & SERVING

The marzipan-decorated cake should not be refrigerated but may be kept at cool room temperature for up to 4 hours.

ADVANCED

MAY DAY DACQUOISE

Photograph, Page 120
Layers of Dacquoise and Almond Genoise filled with sliced strawberries and Cassis Buttercream, surrounded by Japonais, frosted with Cassis Buttercream, and decorated with marzipan violets. Serves 8 to 10

Swirled columns of almond dacquoise, sometimes called "japonais," surround light buttercream-filled dacquoise and genoise layers and form a delightful frame for this bouquet of spring violets.

The almonds must be ground very fine so the dacquoise pipes easily into swirls and layers. These tinted marzipan violets were cut with a ceramicist's tool, a Kemper PCS1 ½-inch pattern cutter, available from the manufacturer by mail (see Sources of Supply). But a small, five-petal flower cutter can be used equally well.

EQUIPMENT

Kemper ½-inch PCS1 pattern cutter or 1-inch, 5-petal flower cutter
Rolling pin
Two kitchen towels or a thin sheet of foam rubber
Cotton swab
One 6-inch round pan
Two baking sheets
Parchment paper
Ateco #0 or #1 round and #32 star tips
Pastry bag
Cardboard round
1 yard lavender satin ribbon, ¼ inch wide
Tweezers

WORK PLAN

Up to 1 day ahead—
Make the marzipan violets, the Almond Genoise, the Dacquoise, and the Cassis Buttercream.
Baking & Preparation—
About 3 hours
Assembly & Decoration—
About 1½ hours, including chilling time

RECIPE

7 ounces marzipan

Violet, pink, and yellow paste food coloring

½ cup confectioners' sugar or cornstarch

½ recipe Nut Genoise, Page 21, made with almonds

1½ recipes Dacquoise, Page 27, made with almonds

1 recipe Cassis Buttercream, Page 28

½ pint strawberries

PREPARATION

1. At least 12 hours ahead, make the marzipan violets. Tint one third of the marzipan violet, one third lavender, and one third pink with violet and pink food coloring. Sprinkle a work surface with confectioners' sugar or cornstarch and knead each piece of marzipan for 30 seconds or longer, until the desired shade is reached. Work with one color at a time, keeping the other marzipan in a covered container to prevent drying out.

2. Roll out the marzipan as thinly as possible and cut out about forty flowers. Mold the flowers and set aside to dry for at least 12 hours.

3. Prepare the genoise batter. Pour enough batter into a 6-inch round pan to fill it halfway. Bake the cake in a preheated oven, testing for doneness after 20 minutes.

4. Trim two sheets of parchment paper to fit the baking sheets. Trace two 6-inch circles on one, and rows of lines 3½ inches apart on the second. Line the baking sheets with the parchment, tracing-side down. Mix the dacquoise. With a #32 tip, pipe the circles within the tracings. With the same tip, pipe about twenty swirled columns, or japonais, within the rows on the second sheet. Bake the dacquoise, switching the position of the baking sheets in the oven halfway through to ensure even baking.

5. Prepare the buttercream.

ASSEMBLY & DECORATION

6. With scissors or a paring knife, trim the dacquoise layers to the same size as the genoise. Using a long serrated knife, slice the genoise in half horizontally. Slice the strawberries.

7. Place one genoise layer on a cardboard round and spread with about ⅓ cup of buttercream, using a metal spatula. Arrange a layer of strawberries over the cream. Position a dacquoise layer over the strawberries and spread with ⅓ cup of buttercream. Place the second dacquoise layer on the cream and spread with ⅓ cup of buttercream. Top with the remaining genoise and refrigerate the cake until the filling is firm—15 to 30 minutes.

8. Frost the cake with buttercream, beginning with the sides and ending with the top. Refrigerate again for 20 to 30 minutes.

9. Frost the cake a second time. The frosting will be completely obscured by the japonais and does not need to be finely finished. Transfer the cake to a serving plate.

10. Position the japonais vertically around the side of the cake, pressing them gently into the

MAY DAY DACQUOISE
·
Recipe, Page 118

P R E T T Y C A K E S

frosting. Tie the ribbon around the japonais to hold them in place.

11. Fill a pastry bag with buttercream. Using the #32 tip, pipe a border of large rosettes around the cake, next to the japonais. Press firmly on the bag, moving in a tight circle to form the rosettes. In the center of the cake, pipe buttercream in concentric circles to form a mounded cushion for the violets.

12. Carefully arrange the violets on the center of the cake within the rosette border. For the last flowers, use tweezers to set them in position.

13. Tint the remaining buttercream with yellow food coloring and spoon it into a pastry bag fitted with a #0 or #1 tip. Pipe three small dots in the center of each violet.

Shaping Marzipan Violets

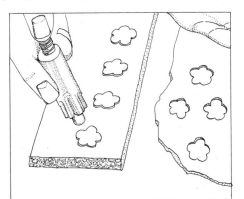

With a Kemper tool or flower cutter, cut out the violets. Place them on folded kitchen towels or a thin sheet of foam rubber and press the ball end of the tool or a cotton swab into the center of each flower, gently twirling the tool back and forth to curve the flower.

Piping Japonais

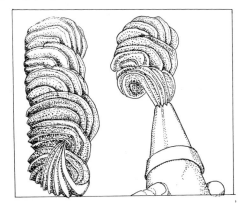

With a #32 tip, pipe twenty swirled columns within rows traced on the parchment. Use maximum pressure to form the fat swirls and at the end of each line, relax the pressure and immediately pull the bag away to finish the column.

STORING & SERVING

Serve the cake immediately or keep it at cool room temperature. Because of the marzipan, the cake should not be refrigerated. Without the violets, the cake may be wrapped loosely in plastic and refrigerated for several hours.

ADVANCED

MOTHER'S DAY CAKE

Photograph, Page 124
Lemon Genoise filled and frosted with Swiss Meringue Buttercream, and decorated with buttercream swirls, marzipan roses and leaves and piping gel.
Serves 8 to 10

The almost rococo design of buttercream ruffs, love-knots, swirls, and rosettes is crowned with a single delicately tinted peach marzipan rose and two rosebuds on this special Mother's Day cake.

The marzipan work should be completed a day or two ahead, but the decorative piping can be done just before serving, and for all its complexity, it is not that demanding. Marzipan leaf presses and cutters are sold at bakers' supply houses and some specialty cookware shops (see Sources of Supply), although the leaves can be cut freehand with a paring knife.

EQUIPMENT

Petal cutter or large decorating tip
1- and 2-inch cutters and leaf press
Rolling pin
Parchment paper
Two 8-inch round pans
Cardboard round
Turntable
Ateco #0 and #3 round, #19 French star, and #102
petal tips
One or two pastry bags
Parchment cone (optional)

WORK PLAN

At least 1 day ahead—
Make the marzipan rose, buds, and leaves.
Up to 1 day ahead—
Bake the Lemon Genoise and prepare the Swiss
Meringue Buttercream.
Baking & Preparation—
About 2½ hours
Assembly & Decoration—
About 2 hours, including chilling time

RECIPE

5 ounces marzipan

¼ cup confectioners' sugar

Red, yellow, brown, and green paste food coloring

1 recipe Lemon Genoise, Page 21

1½ recipes Swiss Meringue Buttercream, Page 27

2 tablespoons piping gel

PREPARATION

1. At least one day ahead, make the marzipan roses and leaves. Color 4 ounces of marzipan a soft peach by combining red, yellow, and a little brown coloring. Tint 1 ounce of marzipan pale green with green and a dab of brown coloring.

2. The marzipan rose and buds are made by pressing individual petals around a cone, following the general instructions on page 74. Keep your hands and work surface dusted with confectioners' sugar to prevent sticking. To make the buds, pinch the edge of the circle three-quarters

around to simulate the rose's characteristic wavy edges. Very lightly dampen the unpressed base edge of the petal with cold water, and attach the base of the petal to the top third of the cone. Wrap the petal around the cone, pressing in gently around the top of the petal, and extending it above the cone. Overlap the petal where it meets, pinching in the bottom slightly. With scissors or a knife, cut off the bottom of the bud and allow to dry on parchment.

3. Make the rose from an inner petal, a second row of three petals, and an outer row of four petals. For the look of a fuller, more mature rose, make the cone a little thicker and the petals slightly larger. Turn out the tips of the inner petals after adding them to the cone. Before attaching the outer row of petals to the rose, place each in the palm of one hand and lightly impress the center with your thumb to cup it. Center the outer row over the inner petals, beginning where the last one ended. Gently pinch the top of the petal when it is in position, and fan the petals outward, overlapping them slightly. Clip off the base of the cone with scissors and dry the rose on parchment.

4. Shape one small and three large leaves with the cutters and leaf press. See page 147 for instructions. Twist each leaf slightly for a natural look, then allow to dry on parchment.

5. Bake the genoise in two 8-inch round pans and prepare the buttercream.

ASSEMBLY & DECORATION

6. Place one layer on a cardboard round. Spread it with about ½ cup of buttercream, using a metal spatula. Top with the second layer and refrigerate until the filling is firm—15 to 30 minutes.

7. Reserve 2 cups of buttercream for decoration. Frost the cake with half the remaining buttercream, beginning with the sides and ending at the top. Refrigerate for 20 minutes.

8. Frost the cake a second time and refrigerate for at least 20 minutes before decorating.

9. To begin the decoration, tint the piping gel with green and brown coloring. Spoon it into a pastry bag fitted with a #0 tip or a small parchment cone with a tiny opening.

10. Set the cake on a turntable and mark guides for the gel pattern, using a toothpick. Start the pattern from the center and repeat it in each quarter of the top. Holding the bag about 1 inch from the cake, pipe the loop, then the curve, and return to the center.

11. Lightly brush any confectioners' sugar from the rose and buds. Center the rose in the gel filigree. Place the rosebuds in front and add the leaves, with the smaller leaf in front.

12. To design the top piping, mark ten evenly spaced scallops. Spoon buttercream into a pastry bag fitted with a #102 tip and pipe the ruffles.

13. In the center of each ruffle, pipe the rosette shapes with a #19 tip.

14. Trace a freeform filigree design on the side of the cake. With a #3 round tip, pipe over the tracing, holding the bag close to the cake.

15. Transfer the cake to a serving plate. With the #19 tip, pipe a border of large individual rosettes around the base of the cake.

Piping the Ruffle Border

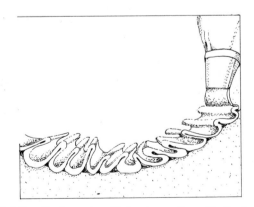

Holding the bag at a 45-degree angle, with the broad opening of the tip at the bottom, pipe the ruffles. Move the bag in a narrow back-and-forth motion, tapping the wider end on the cake with each outer move.

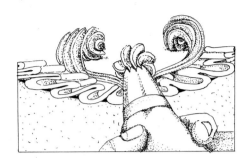

Using a #19 tip, pipe the rosettes inside the ruffles in three stages. Beginning at one end of the semicircle, pipe a rosette with medium pressure, gradually releasing the pressure as you move the bag to the center. Repeat for the other side. Pipe a single round rosette in the center.

STORING & SERVING

The cake may be served immediately or refrigerated for several hours. The marzipan roses should be added just before serving.

PHI BETA KAPPA CAKE

Photograph, Page 125
Almond Genoise filled with apricot preserves and Lemon Buttercream, frosted and decorated with Lemon Buttercream. Serves 18 to 20

For a large graduation party, this cake captures the formality of the occasion without being stuffy. Graceful ribbons and bands of buttercream flutter over and around the cake, held together by bunches of buttercream ivy leaves. To retain a lightness, the ribbons, bands, and leaves are piped in a freeform manner: the wider bands are piped with gentle curves, the smaller ribbons as loose curls.

Under the frosting of Lemon Buttercream lie thin layers of Almond Genoise. To handle such large, thinly sliced layers, use a baking sheet under each layer for support.

MOTHER'S DAY CAKE
·
Recipe, Page 121

PHI BETA KAPPA CAKE

Recipe, Page 123

EQUIPMENT

Two 12-inch round pans
Cardboard round
Turntable
Ateco #5 and #8 round, #61 and #59 petal, #67,
#68, and #69 leaf, and #101 and #103 rose tips
One or two pastry bags

WORK PLAN

Up to 1 day ahead—
Bake the Nut Genoise prepare the Lemon
Buttercream, and strain the preserves.
Baking & Preparation—
About 1½ hours
Assembly & Decoration—
About 2 hours, including chilling time

RECIPE

2 recipes Nut Genoise, Page 21, made with almonds

2 recipes Lemon Buttercream, Page 28

2 cups strained apricot preserves

PREPARATION

1. Bake the genoise in two 12-inch round pans.
Prepare the buttercream.

ASSEMBLY & DECORATION

2. When the cake has cooled, slice each layer
horizontally into thirds, using a long serrated
knife. Place one layer on a cardboard round. With
a metal spatula, spread the cake with ½ cup of
preserves, then ¾ cup of buttercream. Place a
second layer on the cream and spread with preserves and buttercream. Top with a third layer
and spread with only buttercream. Add the fourth
and fifth layers, spreading each with preserves
and buttercream. Top with the final layer and
smooth any filling that has seeped out the sides.
Refrigerate the cake for 20 to 30 minutes to set
the filling.

3. Set aside 1½ cups of buttercream for decoration. Frost the cake with half the remaining
buttercream, beginning with the sides and ending

at the top. Refrigerate the cake about 20 minutes
to set the frosting

4. Frost the cake a second time and refrigerate
for 20 minutes, or until you are ready to decorate.

5. To begin the decoration, set the cake on a
turntable and spoon buttercream into a pastry bag
fitted with a #61 tip. From two points pipe the
ribbons. Use tips #103, #5, #8 and #59 to pipe
additional designs as indicated in illustration
instructions.

6. Three different size leaves will "hold" the ribbons together. With a #69 tip, pipe a wreath of
leaves pointing outward over the points where
the bands meet, leaving a 1-inch opening in the
center. Change to a #68 tip and pipe smaller
leaves over the wreath, slightly closing the space.
With a #67 tip, pipe small leaves over the center
of the wreath and more leaves spilling up and out
from the wreath.

7. Transfer the cake to a serving platter. With a
#101 tip, pipe a wavy border around the base of
the cake. Holding the bag at a slight angle to the
cake, press to form the fold, then release to pull
away and repeat.

Piping Ribbons and Bands

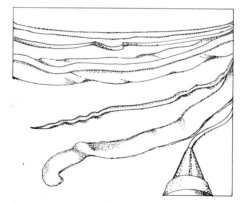

*Set cake on turntable. Using a pastry bag fitted with a
#61 tip, pipe the ribbon design from two points—the
larger at 4 o'clock and the smaller at 11 o'clock. From
each point pipe several wide, flat ribbons stretching
over the top edges and down the sides, working in both
directions. Use a #103 tip to pipe swags between the
shorter bands, a #5 tip to pipe wavy lines between the
swags, a #8 tip to pipe additional wavy lines, and a
#59 tip to pipe over the bands on the sides and edges.*

STORING & SERVING

The cake may be refrigerated for several hours, but it should sit at room temperature for 30 minutes to soften the frosting.

ADVANCED

FATHER'S DAY CAKE

Photograph, Page 128
Coffee Genoise filled and frosted with Chocolate Mousse flavored with Grand Marnier, decorated with chocolate rolls and fondant banners with gel lettering.
Serves 12 to 16

For this holiday, we've spared the flowers and ruffles and created this decidedly masculine cake. A Coffee Genoise smothered with Chocolate Mousse bristles with dark chocolate rolls in a strikingly unconventional, almost architectural, dessert. Making the 125 cigarettes takes time, but don't be disheartened—like chocolate curls, they may be prepared several days in advance and stored in a tightly-covered container. In this case, the chocolate should be tempered so that it doesn't "bloom"—develop a dusty, powdery look—and remains dark, shiny, and crisp. If you don't have enough baking sheets and jelly roll pans for spreading the chocolate, make the rolls in two batches.

The message is written in brown piping gel on flags cut from white rolled fondant (or marzipan or pastillage) and wedged among the rolls just before serving.

EQUIPMENT

Eight baking sheets and/or jelly roll pans
Metal pastry scraper
Two 8-inch round pans
Ateco #0 round tip and pastry bag or parchment cone
Kitchen towel

WORK PLAN

Up to 2 days ahead—
Make the fondant flags and the chocolate rolls.
Up to 1 day ahead—
Bake the Coffee Genoise and prepare and chill the Chocolate Mousse.
Baking & Preparation—
About 4 hours

Assembly & Decoration—
About 2 hours, including chilling time

RECIPE

3 ounces Rolled Fondant, Page 33

½ cup confectioners' sugar

4 pounds semisweet chocolate

1 recipe Coffee Genoise, Page 21

1 recipe Chocolate Mousse, Page 32, flavored with Grand Marnier

2 tablespoons piping gel

Brown liquid food coloring

PREPARATION

1. One or two days ahead, prepare the fondant flags. Sprinkle a work surface with confectioners' sugar and roll out the fondant to a ¼ inch thickness. Use a paring knife to cut three flags ranging in length from 2 to 4 inches and each about 1½ inches wide. Cut the ends on a slight diagonal. Let the flags dry at room temperature for at least a day.

2. For the chocolate rolls, melt the chocolate in two batches according to the instructions on page 70. Using a metal pastry scraper, spread the chocolate onto eight clean, ungreased baking sheets and jelly roll pans evenly to a ⅛ inch thickness. Refrigerate the chocolate until it sets—15 to 20 minutes.

3. Allow the chocolate to sit at room temperature for 5 to 10 minutes. Using the pastry scraper, scrape the chocolate into 3- and 4-inch rolls, about 125 in all. Refrigerate the rolls to set them. To keep them for more than a couple of hours, store the rolls in a tightly covered container in a cool, dry place.

4. Bake the genoise in two 8-inch round pans. Prepare the mousse and flavor it with Grand Marnier.

FATHER'S DAY CAKE

Recipe, Page 127

PRETTY CAKES

5. When the cake has cooled, place one layer on a cardboard round and spread with about ½ cup of mousse, using a metal spatula. Top with the second layer, and refrigerate the cake for 15 to 20 minutes.

6. Frost the cake with the remaining mousse. Since the mousse will be completely covered by the chocolate rolls, the frosting need not be neatly finished. Refrigerate the cake until the mousse is chilled and you are ready to decorate it.

7. Heap about 2 teaspoons of confectioners' sugar onto a plate. Dip one end of each roll into the sugar to give the tip a frosted look. Gently press rolls into the mousse around the sides of the cake, frosted end up. Bunch several rolls together and press them into the top of the cake. Continue adding rolls, building height to the cake with the longest rolls.

8. Tint the piping gel with brown food coloring. Lightly trace the lettering on the flags and lay them on a kitchen towel for stability. Spoon the gel into a pastry bag fitted with a #0 tip or a parchment cone with a tiny opening. Pipe the lettering on the flags. Carefully insert the flags between the rolls.

Shaping Chocolate Rolls

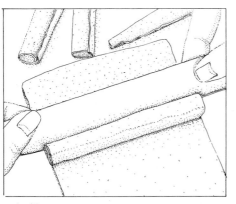

Using a knife or pastry scraper, scrape about 2 inches of chocolate into a tight roll. Make the rolls in lengths of 3 and 4 inches. If the chocolate becomes too warm to work, refrigerate it briefly before continuing.

Before the flags are inserted, the cake may be refrigerated for up to 4 hours. Because they are fragile, add the flags at the last moment. Cut the cake into thin slices with a long, sharp knife, and serve each portion with two or three rolls.

INTERMEDIATE

CHOCOLATE FIREWORKS

Photograph, Page 132
Almond Orange Cake frosted with Chocolate Confectioners' Sugar Frosting and decorated with chocolate stars and chocolate strands. Serves 8 to 10

A riot of dark and milk chocolate shooting stars makes this cake a memorable part of a July 4th celebration. The Almond Orange Cake is baked in a deep rectangular pan (a lasagna pan is perfect) that has been tilted in the oven to create an unusual, slanted cake.

Ateco makes star cutters ranging from 1 to 4 inches across, or you may use star-shaped cookie cutters. Unless the room is exceptionally warm, the stars will not need refrigeration after cutting. They can be made ahead and stored between layers of waxed paper in a tightly covered container in a cool place.

EQUIPMENT

Two or three baking sheets or jelly roll pans
Parchment paper
1-, 2-, 3-, and 4-inch star cutters
Baker's comb (optional)
One 9- by 12-inch pan, about 3-inches deep

WORK PLAN

Up to 1 week ahead—
Make the chocolate stars.
Up to 1 day ahead—
Bake the Almond Orange Cake and prepare the Chocolate Confectioners' Sugar Frosting.
Baking & Preparation—
About 2½ hours
Assembly & Decoration—
About 1½ hours, including chilling time

RECIPE

10 ounces semisweet chocolate

8 ounces milk chocolate

1 recipe Almond Orange Cake, Page 22

1 recipe Chocolate Confectioners' Sugar Frosting, Page 29

PREPARATION

1. Melt 8 ounces each of semisweet and milk chocolate and pour the chocolate on flat, ungreased baking sheets and jelly roll pans. Use a metal pastry scraper to spread the chocolate to a ⅛ inch thickness, but do not overwork by spreading it back and forth more than necessary.

2. Let the chocolate cool until set but still tacky, about 5 minutes. A fingertip pressed against the chocolate should leave a print but not remove any of the chocolate. Run a baker's comb in random swirls over half the chocolate, using both the wide- and medium-toothed sides. Refrigerate the chocolate until it sets—about 15 minutes.

3. Allow the chocolate to sit at room temperature for 5 to 10 minutes. Using star cookie cutters, cut out about two dozen stars. Briefly chill the chocolate before removing the stars from the sheets. Use a small spatula to help remove the stars, if necessary.

4. Mix the cake. Pour the batter into a lightly buttered and floured 9- by 12-inch pan. To give the cake a slope, bake the cake with one end of the pan resting on an inverted ½-cup measuring cup or a 2-inch deep pan. Cover the thinner half of the cake with foil after 20 minutes to prevent overbrowning. Test the cake for doneness near the thickest part after 30 minutes.

5. Prepare the frosting.

ASSEMBLY & DECORATION

6. When the cake is cool, place it on a piece of cardboard cut to fit on a flat serving plate. With a metal spatula, cover the cake with about 1½ cups of frosting, beginning with the sides and ending with the top. Refrigerate the cake until the frosting is firm—15 to 30 minutes.

7. Frost the cake a second time and refrigerate again for 20 to 30 minutes.

8. For the chocolate strands, melt the remaining 2 ounces of semisweet chocolate. Dip a fork in the chocolate, turning it until the tines are heavily coated. Holding the fork over one corner of the thin wedge of the cake, make short, sharp, flicking movements with your wrist to throw the chocolate strands diagonally over the cake. Use a spatula to smooth the chocolate that drizzles down the sides.

9. Set the stars into the cake, starting with the larger stars on a corner of the thick end of the cake. Press the stars into the frosting to anchor them, and lay several flat on the cake.

Cutting Chocolate Stars

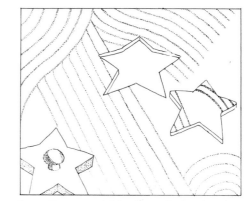

Press the cutters completely through the chocolate. Return the chocolate to the refrigerator for one or two minutes to set, then gently lift off the stars with a small metal spatula.

STORING & SERVING

The cake may be refrigerated, loosely wrapped in plastic, for a day. It can sit at room temperature for two or three hours.

HARVEST MOON CAKE

Photograph, Page 133
Genoise sprinkled with rum, filled and frosted with
Chestnut Buttercream, decorated with raspberry
preserve glaze, pomegranate seeds, chestnuts in syrup,
and set in a grapevine wreath garnished with seasonal
fruit and dried flowers. Serves 8 to 10

Set within a fruit-laden grapevine wreath, this cake captures the spirit of the fall harvest. A light, buttery genoise is filled with buttercream that is enhanced by the subtle, lingering sweetness of chestnut puree, while a sprinkling of rum between each layer cuts the sweetness and adds a slight punch to the flavors. Sweetened chestnut puree is sold in jars or cans. The rosy gloss on top of the cake is a raspberry preserve glaze, produced by spreading boiling preserves directly on the cake. Do this as quickly as possible because as the glaze cools, it will set and show the marks of the spatula.

EQUIPMENT

Two 8-inch round pans
Cardboard round
Ateco #5 round tip
Pastry bag
Grapevine wreath with 10-inch center
Dried flowers

WORK PLAN

Up to 1 day ahead—
Bake the Genoise and prepare the chestnut buttercream.
Up to 12 hours ahead—
Fill and glaze the cake.
Baking & Preparation—
About 1½ hours
Assembly & Decoration—
About 2 hours, including chilling time

RECIPE

1 recipe Genoise, Page 20

1 recipe Swiss Meringue Buttercream, Page 27

10 ounces sweetened chestnut puree

½ cup rum

1 cup raspberry preserves

9 whole chestnuts, in syrup

3 small pomegranates

1 pound champagne grapes

2 Seckel pears

1 red Bartlett pear

PREPARATION

1. Bake the genoise in two 8-inch round pans.

2. Prepare the buttercream. Add 8 ounces of puree to 1½ cups of buttercream for the filling, and tint the remaining 2½ cups of buttercream with 2 ounces of puree.

ASSEMBLY & DECORATION

3. When the cake layers are cool, use a long serrated knife to slice them in half horizontally. Place one layer on a cardboard round and sprinkle it with about 2 tablespoons of rum. Using a metal spatula, spread the cake with about ½ cup of chestnut buttercream and position a second layer on top. Repeat this procedure until all the layers are filled, topping with the fourth layer. Sprinkle this with the remaining rum and refrigerate the cake until the filling is firm—15 to 30 minutes.

4. To prepare the glaze, heat the raspberry preserves in a small saucepan. Bring to a boil, strain, and boil again. Immediately pour the preserves onto the top of the cake, spreading rapidly and evenly with a metal spatula. Smooth any glaze that runs down the sides of the cake.

5. Frost the sides of the cake with a thin layer of tinted buttercream. Refrigerate until firm—20 to 30 minutes.

6. Frost the sides a second time and refrigerate again for 20 to 30 minutes.

7. Spoon buttercream into a pastry bag fitted with a #5 tip. Pipe a bead border around the top of the cake at alternating angles, pivoting your

CHOCOLATE FIREWORKS
·
Recipe, Page 129

HARVEST MOON CAKE

Recipe, Page 131

wrists as you change the position of the bag to create a feathered effect. Pipe a second border directly over the first.

8. Decorate the top of the cake with chestnuts interspersed with groupings of seeds from one pomegranate.

STORING & SERVING

The decorated cake may be refrigerated, uncovered, for up to 12 hours and removed from the refrigerator about 30 minutes before serving. Decorate the wreath with dried flowers and fresh fruit up to 12 hours before the cake is to be served.

SIMPLE

THE HALLOWEEN CAKE

Photograph, Page 136
Orange Layer Cake filled with Confectioners' Sugar
Frosting and M & M's, frosted with Confectioners'
Sugar Frosting and decorated with black gel cats.
Serves 14 to 16

Yellow-eyed black cats stalk over the top and around the sides of this spooky Halloween cake. A cat cookie cutter, about 3 inches long, is used to impress the outline for the black cats on the top of the cake; they are sold in most bakers' or cookware stores. We added eyes and fur on the tails.

EQUIPMENT

Two 9-inch square pans
3-inch cat cutter
Ateco #0 round tip and pastry bag or two parchment cones

WORK PLAN

Up to 1 day ahead—
Bake the Orange Layer Cake and prepare the Confectioners' Sugar Frosting.
Baking & Preparation—
About 1 hour

Assembly & Decoration—
About 1½ hours, including chilling time

RECIPE

1½ recipes Orange Layer Cake, Page 22

1 recipe Confectioners' Sugar Frosting, Page 29

½ cup plain M & M's

⅓ cup piping gel

Black and yellow paste food coloring

PREPARATION

1. Bake the cake in two 9-inch square pans. Test for doneness after 25 minutes.

2. Prepare the frosting. With a sharp knife or in a food processor fitted with the metal blade, coarsely chop the M & M's. Stir the chocolate pieces into 1 cup of frosting.

ASSEMBLY & DECORATION

3. Place one layer on a cardboard square or flat serving plate. With a metal spatula, spread the cake with the cup of M & M frosting. Position the second layer on top, and smooth any frosting that may have seeped out between the layers. Refrigerate the cake to set the filling—15 to 30 minutes.

4. Frost the cake with about half the remaining frosting, starting with the sides and ending at the top. (See page 13 for detailed frosting instructions.) Refrigerate the cake again for 20 to 30 minutes.

5. Frost the cake a second time with the remaining frosting and refrigerate for another 20 to 30 minutes.

6. Outline the cats on top of the cake with a cat-shaped cookie cutter. Tint ¼ cup of piping gel black. Spoon the black gel into a pastry bag with a #0 tip or a parchment cone with a tiny opening. Pipe the cat outlines and freehand tails. Around the sides of the cake, pipe cats with arched backs.

7. For the cats' eyes, tint the remaining gel yellow. Spoon the gel into another pastry bag with a #0 tip or parchment cone with a small opening. Pipe in the eyes.

Piping Halloween Cats

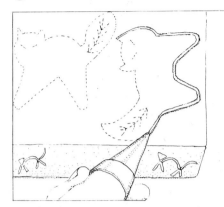

Outline eight cats, lightly impressing the cutter on the chilled frosting. Holding the bag or cone close to the cake, pipe in each outline with black gel. Then fill in the tails and eyes.

STORING & SERVING

The cake may be refrigerated, lightly wrapped in plastic, for up to 1 day. Remove from the refrigerator about 30 minutes before serving to allow the frosting to soften.

SIMPLE

HEARTLAND THANKSGIVING CAKE

Photograph, Page 137
Nut Cake filled with apricot preserves and Confectioners' Sugar Frosting, frosted with Confectioners' Sugar Frosting, and decorated with dried apricots, pecans, and Brazil nuts. Serves 8 to 10

A pleasing alternative to the more traditional pumpkin and pecan pies, this cake is designed to reflect the simple virtues celebrated at Thanksgiving. It's made with pecans, one of the few nuts indigenous to this country, and is simply decorated with dried apricots and shelled pecans. Very American, and very elegant—a perfect dessert to serve after the Thanksgiving feast.

EQUIPMENT

Two 8-inch round pans

WORK PLAN

Up to 1 day ahead—
Bake the Nut Cake and prepare the Confectioners' Sugar Frosting.
Baking & Preparation—
About 1¼ hours
Assembly & Decoration—
About 1 hour, including chilling time

RECIPE

1 recipe Nut Cake, Page 24, made with pecans

1 recipe Confectioners' Sugar Frosting, Page 29

3 tablespoons apricot preserves

6 dried apricot halves

2 ounces (about ½ cup) pecan halves

4 or 5 Brazil nuts

PREPARATION

1. Bake the cake in two 8-inch round pans. Prepare the frosting.

ASSEMBLY & DECORATION

2. When the cake is cool, place one layer on a flat serving plate or cardboard round. With a metal spatula, spread the layer with apricot preserves. Spread about ½ cup of frosting over the preserves, and position the second layer on top. Smooth any frosting that may have seeped out the sides, and refrigerate the cake to set the filling—15 to 30 minutes.

3. Frost the cake with about half the remaining frosting, beginning with the sides and ending with the top. (For detailed frosting instructions, see page 13.) Refrigerate the cake again for 20 to 30 minutes.

4. Frost the cake a second time. To form the swirls, use a metal spatula that has been warmed in hot water, then dried. Work outward from one point, creating a ripple effect across the top of the cake. Refrigerate the cake until ready to decorate.

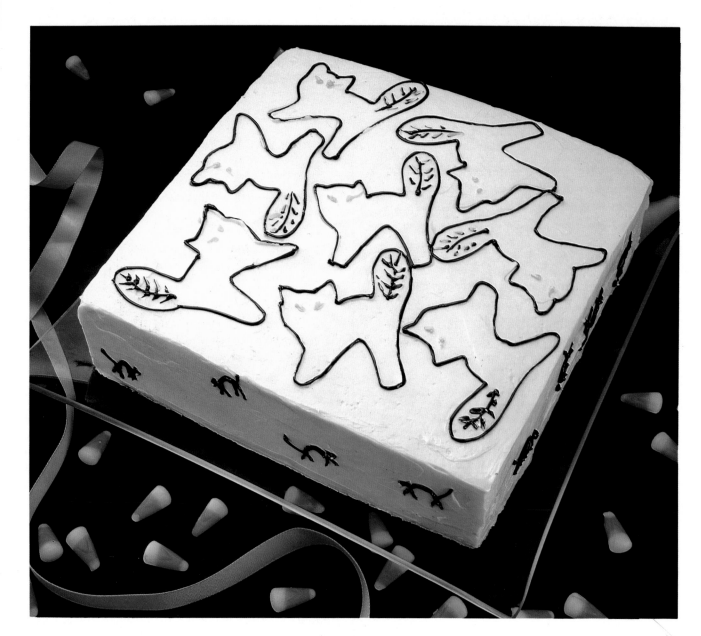

THE HALLOWEEN CAKE
·
Recipe, Page 134

HEARTLAND THANKSGIVING CAKE

Recipe, Page 135

5. Cut the apricot halves in half. Press the apricots and nuts into the frosting, beginning where the swirls meet and fanning out across the top and sides of the cake. Break up a few pecans and set the small pieces so that they seem to be tumbling off the cake.

STORING & SERVING

The cake may be served immediately or refrigerated for several hours. Allow it to sit at room temperature for 30 minutes before serving.

SIMPLE

BRANDIED CHRISTMAS FRUITCAKE

Photograph, Page 140
Fruitcake glazed with apricot preserves and decorated with glacéed dried fruits and unshelled nuts.
Serves 8 to 10

Rich fruitcake is true Christmas fare, and this version is both traditional and innovative. Lighter than most fruitcakes and intriguingly spicy, the cake's texture is seen through a gloss of apricot preserves. An abundance of glistening glacéed fruits and unshelled nuts completes the simple yet effective decoration for the cake.

Bearing in mind hectic holiday schedules, the cake and fruits can be prepared well in advance and assembled virtually on the spur of the moment. As with most fruitcakes, this one will improve with aging, giving the spices, fruit, and brandy a chance to mature. Still, the recipe does not require aging and the cake is delicious just after baking. Use whatever nuts and fruit are available but keep in mind that a variety will add color and interest to the cake. For more color, a few sprigs of pine are set in the fruit wreath just before serving.

EQUIPMENT

One 6-inch round pan, 3½ inches deep
Large serving platter
Small pine branch

WORK PLAN

Up to 4 months ahead—
Bake the Fruitcake.
Up to 1 day ahead—
Make the Stock Syrup and glacé the fruits.
Baking & Preparation—
4 hours, including resting time
Assembly & Decoration—
About 20 minutes

RECIPE

1 recipe Fruitcake, Page 25

About 45 pieces dried fruits: apples, apricots, dates, figs, peaches, papayas

3 recipes Stock Syrup, Page 34

½ cup apricot preserves

18 to 24 unshelled nuts: almonds, walnuts, Brazil nuts, hazelnuts

PREPARATION

1. Bake the cake in a 6-inch round pan.

2. To prepare the dried fruit, place a rack over a sheet of parchment or waxed paper. Prepare the stock syrup and bring to a boil in a large saucepan. Submerge the dried fruits in the syrup, ten or twelve at a time, and simmer until they are translucent and glistening—2 to 3 minutes. Remove with tongs and spread on the rack to dry for 1½ to 2 hours, or overnight.

ASSEMBLY & DECORATION

3. Place the cake on a serving plate large enough to hold the fruit-and-nut garnish. Heat the apricot preserves in a small saucepan just until they begin to boil. Strain them. Brush the preserves over the top and sides of the cake. Pile the glacéed fruits and unshelled nuts around the cake, pressing some into the preserves.

STORING & SERVING

The assembled fruitcake can be kept at room temperature for up to 4 hours. Just before serving, add the pine garnish.

MIDNIGHT YULE LOG

Photograph, Page 141
Chocolate Genoise sprinkled with kirsch, filled with cherry preserves and Butter Ganache, frosted with Butter Ganache, and decorated with chocolate bark and confectioners' sugar. Serves 8 to 10

The night-dark richness of this log is accentuated by a flurry of snow-white confectioners' sugar. Beneath the chocolate bark, a sprinkling of kirsch and a kiss of sour cherry preserves heighten the deliciously intense chocolate flavor. The Christmas Log, or Buche de Noel, is a traditional French holiday dessert, its shape signifying the comfort of the log in the fireplace.

EQUIPMENT

One 11½- by 15½-inch jelly roll pan
Two baking sheets or jelly roll pans
Metal pastry scraper
Fine sieve
Parchment paper
Sprigs of holly (optional)

WORK PLAN

Up to 2 days ahead—
Make the chocolate bark.
Up to 1 day ahead—
Bake the Chocolate Genoise and prepare the Butter Ganache.
Baking & Preparation—
About 2 hours
Assembly & Decoration—
About 2 hours, including chilling time

RECIPE

1 pound semisweet chocolate

1 recipe Chocolate Genoise, Page 21

½ cup confectioners' sugar

1 recipe Butter Ganache, Page 30

¼ cup kirsch

¼ cup sour cherry preserves

PREPARATION

1. Several hours ahead, make the chocolate bark. (Refer to the instructions for making chocolate curls on page 70.) Spread the chocolate about ⅛ inch thick and chill. When it is set, scrape the chocolate into half curls that will resemble bark.

2. Bake the genoise in a jelly roll pan. While the cake is still cooling in the pan, sprinkle confectioners' sugar over a kitchen towel or parchment paper one or two inches wider than the cake. Turn the warm cake out onto the towel or paper and sprinkle with sugar. Starting from a longer side, roll the cake fairly tightly, using the towel or paper for support. (For illustrated directions, see page 43.) Set aside the rolled cake, wrapped in the towel or paper, to cool completely.

3. Prepare the ganache.

ASSEMBLY & DECORATION

4. Unroll the cake and sprinkle it with the kirsch. Using a metal spatula, spread with cherry preserves and about 1 cup of ganache. Reroll the cake, and refrigerate until the filling is firm—15 to 30 minutes.

5. Frost the cake with ganache, reserving about ½ cup for decorating. Refrigerate again for 15 to 20 minutes.

6. Using a long serrated knife, slice off about one-third of the roll with a diagonal cut. Cut this smaller piece diagonally in half to form two angled pieces or "knots." Transfer the cake to a flat serving plate. Position one knot on top of the roll and the other at the side. Press gently to secure them in place, and smooth the ganache.

7. Frost both ends of the cake and the knots with ganache. Warm the spatula in hot water, then dry, to smooth the frosting.

8. Place strips of bark on the cake. Using your fingers and a small spatula, press the bark into the ganache.

9. Just before serving, dust one side of the log with confectioners' sugar. Garnish with holly.

BRANDIED CHRISTMAS FRUITCAKE

Recipe, Page 138

PRETTY CAKES

MIDNIGHT YULE LOG

Recipe, Page 139

Dusting With Confectioners' Sugar

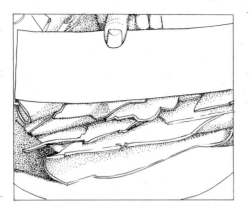

Just before serving, dust one side of the log with confectioners' sugar. Slip paper under one side of the cake to protect the plate. Holding the sieve 4 to 5 inches above the log, lightly sieve sugar over the side of the log.

STORING & SERVING

The cake can be refrigerated for up to 1 day, but allow it to sit at room temperature for 30 minutes to soften the ganache before serving.

ADVANCED

WHITE CHOCOLATE BUCHE DE NOEL

Photograph, Page 144
Genoise filled with Praline Buttercream, frosted with Swiss Meringue Buttercream, decorated with white chocolate curls and confectioners' sugar, and garnished with pine cones and sprigs of fir. Serves 8 to 10

White chocolate is preferred by many people for its smoother, creamier flavor and here it adds a sumptuous yet almost ethereal quality to a Christmas buche. Beneath the buttercream frosting is a light genoise filled with buttercream, spiked with ground praline. Fronds of dark green fir and pine cones contrast prettily with the creamy whiteness of the cake.

Although technically not chocolate, white chocolate behaves in much the same way as milk or dark chocolate varieties, however, after melting it should be strained before spreading to remove any tiny lumps that often appear.

EQUIPMENT

Strainer
Three baking sheets
Metal pastry scraper
One 11½- by 15½-inch jelly roll pan
Ateco #2 round tip
Pastry bag
Fine sieve

WORK PLAN

Up to 2 days ahead—
Make the white chocolate curls.
Up to 1 day ahead—
Bake the Genoise and prepare the Swiss Meringue Buttercream.
Baking & Preparation—
About 2 hours
Assembly & Decoration—
About 2 hours, including chilling time

RECIPE

1 pound white chocolate

1 recipe Genoise, Page 20

½ cup confectioners' sugar

1 recipe Swiss Meringue Buttercream, Page 27

¼ cup ground Praline, Page 34

PREPARATION

1. Several hours ahead, make the white chocolate curls. Refer to the directions for making chocolate curls on page 70, and strain the melted chocolate before spreading it on the baking sheets. When it is set, scrape the chocolate into short curls about 2 inches wide.

2. Bake the genoise in a jelly roll pan. While the cake is still cooling in the pan, sprinkle confectioners' sugar over a kitchen towel or parchment paper one or two inches wider than the cake. Turn the warm cake out onto the towel or paper and sprinkle with sugar. Starting from a longer side, roll the cake fairly tightly, using the towel or paper for support. (For illustrated directions, see page 43.) Set aside the rolled cake, wrapped in the towel or paper, to cool completely.

3. Prepare the buttercream. Beat the ground praline into 1 cup of buttercream for the filling.

ASSEMBLY & DECORATION

4. Unroll the cake onto the parchment or towel. With a metal spatula, spread the praline buttercream over the cake. Reroll the cake, and refrigerate it until the filling is firm—15 to 20 minutes.

5. Frost the cake with buttercream, reserving ½ cup for decoration. Refrigerate the cake again for 20 to 30 minutes.

6. Cut a 2-inch piece from one end of the cake, slicing it on the diagonal. Transfer the cake to a flat serving plate. Position the "knot" on top of the roll, then press gently to secure the knot and smooth the buttercream around it. Trim the other end of the cake diagonally for symmetry.

7. Spoon the remaining buttercream into a pastry bag fitted with a #2 tip. Pipe a spiral of frosting on the exposed end of the knot to simulate the rings of a cut log. Pipe frosting in semicircles of decreasing size on both ends of the cake.

8. Place white chocolate curls over the cake, leaving the decorated ends uncovered. Just before serving, sift the confectioners' sugar over the cake, holding the sieve 4 to 5 inches from the cake.

Shaping a Buche

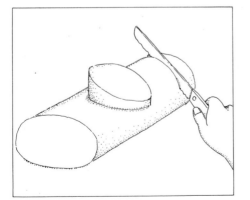

Using a long, serrated knife, cut a diagonal slice 2 inches from one end of the cake. Position the knot on top of the roll, slightly off center and toward one end. Trim the other end of the cake diagonally for symmetry.

STORING & SERVING

The cake may be refrigerated, without the sifted confectioners' sugar, for up to 1 day, but should be allowed to sit at room temperature for 30 minutes to soften. Just before serving, decorate the plate with pine cones and sprigs of fir.

ADVANCED

CHRISTMAS GOLD CAKE

Photograph, Page 145
Spice Cake sprinkled with rum, filled and frosted with orange marmalade, covered with marzipan and gold leaf, and decorated with marzipan holly leaves and red gel. Serves 8 to 10.

This is real gold shimmering on our ultimate Christmas cake—the pure 22 karat kind. The thinnest veneer of gold leaf is layered over marzipan for what is surely the last word in "rich" frostings. Be sure to use only 22 karat—the purest—gold leaf. It comes in packets of 25 sheets about 2 inches square, available in art supply stores for about $25. The layer of gold is extremely thin, totally without flavor, and absolutely harmless.

The marzipan holly is fragile, and we suggest making several extra leaves in case of breakage. The berries are red piping gel, but both the leaves and berries can be replaced with the real holly and berries.

EQUIPMENT

Leaf cutter and press
Baking sheet
Two 8-inch round pans
Cardboard round
Pastry brush
Parchment paper

WORK PLAN

Up to 3 days ahead—
Make the marzipan holly.
Up to 2 days ahead—
Bake the Spice Cake, cover with marzipan, and apply the gold leaf.
Up to 1 day ahead—
Decorate the cake with leaves and berries.

WHITE CHOCOLATE BUCHE DE NOEL
·
Recipe, Page 142

PRETTY CAKES

CHRISTMAS GOLD CAKE
·
Recipe, Page 143

Baking & Preparation—
About 1¼ hours
Assembly & Decoration—
About 1¼ hours

R E C I P E

21 ounces marzipan

½ cup confectioners' sugar

Green and red paste food coloring

1 recipe Spice Cake, Page 24

2 tablespoons rum

1 cup thin cut orange marmalade

¼ cup piping gel

25 leaves (1 package) 22 karat German gold leaf

P R E P A R A T I O N

1. The marzipan holly leaves will need time to dry, so make them first. Sprinkle a work surface with confectioners' sugar and knead 7 ounces of marzipan with green food coloring until it reaches the desired intensity. Roll out the marzipan to ¹⁄₁₆- to ⅛-inch thick. Cut about thirty-five leaves. Mold each in the press and after removing it, curl it slightly. Set the leaves on a baking sheet dusted with confectioners' sugar and allow them to dry at room temperature for twelve to twenty-four hours.

2. Bake the cake in two 8-inch round pans.

A S S E M B L Y   &   D E C O R A T I O N

3. When the cake has cooled, place one layer on a cardboard round. Brush it with 2 tablespoons of rum. With a metal spatula, spread the cake with ½ cup of orange marmalade. If the marmalade is too thick, warm it gently in a small saucepan over low heat to thin it slightly. Place the second layer on top and refrigerate the cake for 15 minutes to set the filling.

4. With a long serrated knife, bevel the top edge of the cake until it is evenly and smoothly rounded, following the instructions on page 12.

5. Heat the remaining ½ cup of marmalade to thin it and brush it over the top and sides of the cake.

6. Sprinkle a work surface with confectioners' sugar. Roll out the remaining marzipan to a 14-inch circle, about ⅛-inch thick. Center and drape the marzipan over the cake, referring to the instructions on page 77. Gently pat and smooth the marzipan into place, and trim the excess from the bottom with a paring knife. Transfer the cake to a serving plate large enough for the holly leaf border.

7. Brush the marzipan with just a little water, only enough to make it tacky. Starting at the center of the top of the cake, lay a gold leaf, paper side up, on the cake and rub gently with your fingertip to transfer the gold onto the marzipan. Handle the leaves carefully and be sure to touch only the tissue paper backing sheet, not the gold itself or it will come off on your fingers and be wasted. As you work your way over the cake, overlap each leaf slightly to ensure there are no gaps. If you do have uneven areas to cover, lay a leaf over the space and rub the tissue over that area—only the rubbed section will transfer to the cake. The finished effect will not be completely smooth, even the coating of gold but, rather, an antiqued, burnished look.

8. Arrange the marzipan holly leaves in clusters of three as a border around the base of the cake.

9. Tint the ¼-cup of piping gel with red paste coloring. Roll a sheet of parchment paper into a cone, snip a ⅛-inch opening, and fill the cone with gel. Pipe berries onto the marzipan leaves and along the plate. The berries will not harden.

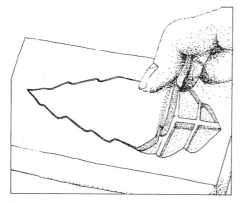

Sprinkle a work surface with confectioners' sugar and roll out the marzipan to about ⅛ to 1/16 inch thick. Using a leaf cutter, cut out about thirty-five holly leaves. Press each one in the leaf press to detail the veins and then use your fingers to curl each one slightly for a realistic look. Set aside to dry.

STORING & SERVING

The cake may be kept at cool room temperature for up to a day, but should not be refrigerated.

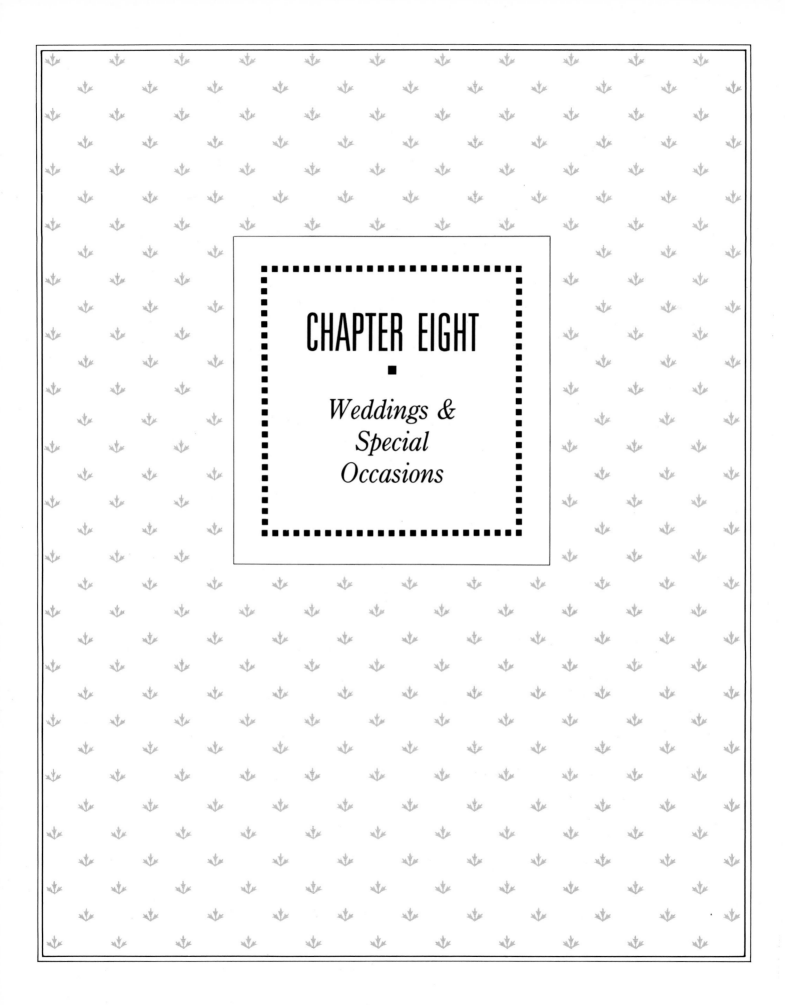

CHAPTER EIGHT

■

*Weddings &
Special
Occasions*

A wedding cake is the baker's *piece de resistance,* serving as the centerpiece at the climax of the celebration. Reflecting the mood and tone the bridal couple have chosen, it may be simply elegant or ornately decorated, an elaborate tower for a grand reception, or a dignified single tier for an intimate circle.

The traditional wedding cake is a multitiered structure with a pristine armor of royal icing. This kind of cake has its advantages. It can be made well in advance and is visually impressive. Unfortunately, its taste frequently does not live up to its appearance and wedding cakes have earned a reputation of being disappointingly bland. But contemporary cakes are as varied as the celebrations themselves and their flavor is considered as important as their beauty. We have tried to cover a range of styles and flavors in the following cakes. Some are traditional in appearance, while others are rather unconventional. The recipes are for cakes of richly flavored genoise, dacquoise, and fruitcake, filled with luscious creams and fresh fruit, frosted with smooth buttercream, ganache, marzipan, or fondant. Decorations are the crowning touch. A harmonious pairing of nuts and leaves, or shiny chocolate leaves and curls bring a casual yet joyful feeling; fresh flowers can be used in countless combinations; and fondant or royal icing flowers will add a sophisticated tone.

The challenge a wedding cake promises may seem overwhelming. But a capable home baker should not be unnecessarily daunted by the thought of making a cake so large, so elaborate, and so important. Good organization and plenty of time are the keys to success. If you are a beginner, consider one of the simpler cakes in this chapter. The more intricate, ornate cakes are best left to advanced bakers who are comfortable with delicate pastry bag techniques and pastillage work.

Assembling a tiered wedding cake requires some consideration of structure and balance. Filled and frosted tiers can be stacked directly on top of each other or separated by plastic columns, but they must be adequately supported. If several tiers were merely stacked one on another, they would gradually sink

In a tiered cake, each tier is anchored on cardboard and supported by three or four wood dowels or plastic straws inserted into the tier below to carry the weight of the higher tier. When the tiers are stacked directly on each other, a long wood dowel is inserted through all the tiers. This dowel acts as an anchor to prevent the movement of the entire structure.

If you wish to anchor the tiers in place, cut a wood skewer or ¼-inch dowel to the full height of the assembled wedding cake. Trim one end of the skewer to a point with a pencil sharpener or sharp knife. Insert the point into the center of the top tier and push it down until it touches the cardboard round under the top tier. Using a hammer, tap the skewer gently but firmly until it pierces the lower cardboard rounds and only ¼ inch remains visible.

More often than not, a wedding cake will have to be transported. With a cake in which the tiers are separated by columns, the tiers should be removed and placed in separate boxes deep enough to hold both the tier and the columns it supports. Don't attempt to separate a cake whose tiers sit directly on top of each other and are firmly anchored together and frosted as one. The cake or tiers should be placed in cardboard boxes and, if you are travelling only a short distance, the boxes can be left open.

In transit, rest the boxes on a flat, nonslippery surface. Soft kitchen towels or aprons should be stuffed around the boxes to keep them from skidding. In summer, it's essential to have an air-conditioned car for transportation, especially if the cake has been frosted with buttercream.

Take everything you need to complete the decoration of the cake—fresh flowers, and leaves, pastillage or fondant flowers, any ornaments for the top of the cake, ribbon and lace—packed in their own boxes. Pack extra frosting with a pastry bag and appropriate tips for last-minute repairs. Remember also to pack a sharp, serrated knife and a spatula for serving the cake in the event that these are not provided. Above all, give yourself plenty of time for both the journey and for assembling the cake at its destination.

When the bride and groom have made the customary first cut, it's a good idea to take the wedding cake behind the scenes to cut it. To serve a tiered cake, first remove the anchors and take off the top tier with a metal spatula. This small "cake" is traditionally given to the bride and groom, to be frozen and enjoyed on their first anniversary. (For this reason, the top tier is sometimes well-aging fruitcake, but any other kind of cake may be kept if frozen properly.)

If the top tier is to be served immediately, place it on a flat surface and remove any decorations, especially those that have been anchored with wire. To serve the larger layers, cut a circle about two inches in from the edge of the cake and then cut small slices from this border. After the first tier is cut, lift it off its cardboard round and cut the larger tier below in the same way.

In the cakes that follow, the yield is estimated on the entire cake, including the top tier. If you want to keep the top tier, subtract between eight and fourteen servings, depending on its size. Wedding cake servings are generally smaller than those from other cakes, and so yields are estimated on moderate portions.

Stacking Tiers With Straws or Chopsticks

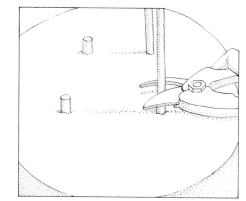

Use pruning scissors to cut four lengths of chopsticks or plastic straws to the height of the cake into which they will be inserted. Insert them into the cake in a square formation. Alternatively, they can be inserted into the cake first and then clipped. The supports will be pressed directly into the cake to touch the base below when the next tier is added.

Separating Tiers With Chopsticks

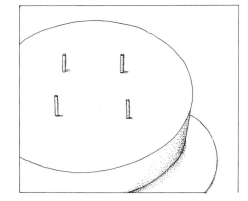

For cakes that require a slight separation of the top layer, allow the supports to extend beyond the surface of the cake.

Stacking Tiers With a Separator Kit

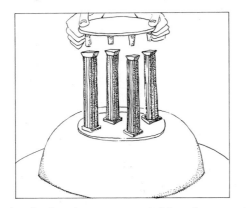

For tiered cakes that are separated by columns, cut the plastic dowels to the height of the tier into which they will be inserted. Insert dowels into the bottom of a plastic separator smaller in size than the cake. Attach four columns to the top of the separator and center separator on top of the cake, pressing dowels as anchors into the cake's surface. Columns will snap into separators. Place a dab of glue atop the separator so that the next cardboard round holding a cake will stay in place.

Adding Tiers to a Cake

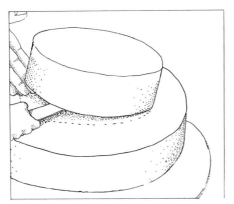

Mark the outline of the next tier on the tier below, perfectly centering it within the circle of the cake tier. Using a metal spatula, gently slip the cake onto the outlined area.

Decorating With Fresh Flowers

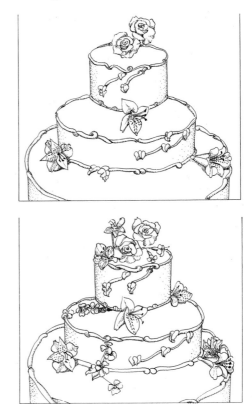

Flowers may be set directly into a cake by their stems, or the stems may be wrapped in straws or aluminum foil. First place large flowers on the important focal points of the cake. Group two or three on the top tier, and place one or two on each successively larger tier. Smaller flowers and leaves fill out the design.

Cutting the Cake

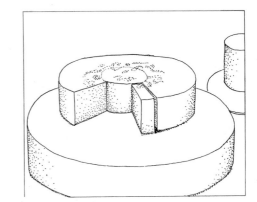

Remove the top tier with a metal spatula and set aside. To slice and serve each layer, cut a circle about 2 inches from the edge of the cake. Cut small slices an inch or more wide from this border. With larger tiers, cut another circle, and slice that into portions. Innermost cake may then be cut into wedges.

LEMON ARBOR WEDDING CAKE
·
Recipe, Page 154

LEMON ARBOR WEDDING CAKE

Photograph, Page 153
Dacquoise filled with Almond Cream, frosted with
Lemon Buttercream, and decorated with crumbled
Dacquoise, hazelnuts, almonds, confectioners' sugar,
lemon leaves, and lemon thyme. Serves 25 to 30

For a small wedding, these octagons of light, crisp dacquoise filled with subtly sweet almond cream make a charming cake. Lemon buttercream, decorated with crumbled dacquoise, nuts, sprigs of lemon thyme, and sifted confectioners' sugar contrast strikingly with the glossy-leaf garnish. Mix the dacquoise with equal amounts of hazelnuts and almonds.

To form the octagonal dacquoise, layers are piped onto octagonal bases cut from parchment paper. Make dacquoise in three batches of one each 8- and 12-inch layers. No supports are needed because of the lightness of the dacquoise. Lemon leaves are available from most florists, or an alternative decoration would be ivy, vinca vine, or any other kind of smallish, dark green leaves.

EQUIPMENT

2 baking sheets
Parchment paper
Ateco #5 large round tip
Pastry bag
Fine sieve
12-inch and 8-inch cardboard rounds
15 lemon leaves
12 sprigs lemon thyme

WORK PLAN

Up to 1 day ahead—
Bake the Dacquoise, and prepare the Almond Cream and Lemon Buttercream.
Up to 1 hour ahead—
Decorate the cake with confectioners' sugar, nuts, leaves, and thyme.
Baking & Preparation—
About 4 hours, plus resting time
Assembly & Decoration—
About 1½ hours, including chilling time

RECIPE

3 recipes Dacquoise, Page 27

2 recipes Lemon Buttercream, Page 28, made with 6 egg yolks

2 recipes Almond Cream, Page 31

1 to 2 cups confectioners' sugar

3 ounces mixed almonds and hazelnuts

PREPARATION

1. Cut three 12-inch and three 8-inch octagons from parchment paper. Line baking sheets with parchment paper and center an 8-inch and 12-inch octagon template on the baking sheets.

2. Make the dacquoise in three batches of one recipe each. Fit a #5 tip in a pastry bag, and pipe the dacquoise onto the parchment octagons, working from the outside so that the shape is clearly defined at the outside edge. On an empty area of the sheet, pipe batter into random shapes, which will be crumbled for decoration. Bake according to the recipe directions.

3. For the buttercream, lightly beat the egg yolks. Prepare the buttercream, and before adding the lemon zest and juice, beat in the yolks. When they are smoothly incorporated, beat in the zest and juice.

4. Prepare the almond cream.

ASSEMBLY & DECORATION

5. When they are cool, carefully lift the dacquoise layers from the parchment paper. With a paring knife or scissors, trim the 12-inch layers so that they are exactly the same size. Repeat for the 8-inch layers.

6. Cut a 12-inch and an 8-inch cardboard round to fit the dacquoise layers. Place a 12-inch dacquoise on the larger round, anchoring it with a dab of buttercream. Generously spread the dacquoise with about 1½ cups of almond cream, using a metal spatula. Position the second 12-inch layer on top, matching the sides of the octagon, and spread with another 1½ cups of almond cream.

Top with the third layer, and smooth any filling that may have seeped out. Repeat the assembly for the 8-inch tiers, spreading about 1 cup of cream between each layer. Refrigerate both cakes until the filling is firm—about 15 minutes.

7. With a metal spatula, frost the sides of both cakes with buttercream, but do not frost the tops. Keep the octagonal shape of each cake clearly defined through the frosting by holding the spatula straight against one side of the octagon and spreading the frosting to the edge. Lift the spatula off the cake and then frost the next side. When all the sides are covered, go back over the edges to smooth and define them. Chill both cakes until the frosting is firm—10 to 15 minutes.

8. Frost the cakes a second time, still keeping the shape defined. Crumble the extra dacquoise shapes into small pieces and press them gently into the sides of the cake in random fashion, clustering them to accentuate the shape of the cakes. Refrigerate for 10 to 15 minutes.

9. To assemble the cake, put a dab of buttercream in the middle of the larger tier and center the smaller tier on it. Press more crumbled dacquoise around the base of the smaller cake to conceal the join.

10. Complete the decoration with a thick layer of sieved confectioners' sugar over the layers. Holding a fine sieve 3 to 4 inches over the cake, carefully cover only the tops of the tiers. Pile all but ten to twelve nuts on top of the cake, nestling them into the sugar. Lay four to six lemon leaves on top of the cake and the others on the bottom tier and around the base of the cake. Randomly distribute the remaining nuts on the cake. Insert the lemon thyme sprigs among the nuts and leaves on top of each tier.

Making Parchment Octagons

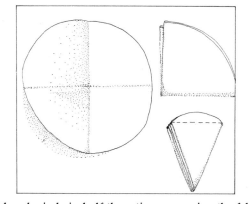

Fold each circle in half three times, creasing the folds so that the sections are flat and even. Trim off the curved, unfolded edge. When opened, the paper will have the shape of an octagon.

STORING & SERVING

The frosted cake, decorated with only crumbled dacquoise, may be tightly covered with plastic wrap and refrigerated overnight. The confectioners' sugar, nuts, leaves, and thyme should be added just before serving.

GARLANDS OF FLOWERS WEDDING CAKE

Recipe, Page 157

GARLANDS OF FLOWERS WEDDING CAKE

Photographs Pages 156, 160
Almond Genoise filled with Grand Marnier, strawberries,
and Almond Buttercream, frosted with Almond Butter-
cream and decorated with garlands of buttercream
flowers and leaves and fresh flowers. Serves 70

The sweet, subtle flavor of almonds is the keynote of this cool, fresh-looking wedding cake. The cake itself is almond genoise, filled with almond buttercream. Sliced fresh strawberries between the layers provide a pleasing contrast, and the flavor is further enhanced with a sprinkling of Grand Marnier. For extra smoothness, the cake is frosted with three coatings of buttercream and is decorated with delicately piped garlands of flowers and leaves, deliberately free-form and flowing, to give the cake its fresh, natural look. The finished cake is decorated with flowers of your choice. The warm apricot and peach tones of calla lilies and hermanthius lilies make the cake perfect for an autumn wedding, while the soft lavenders and pinks make the cake equally appropriate for a spring or summer wedding.

Before filling, the genoise layers are sliced in half horizontally. To avoid breaking these thin, delicate cakes, always use a flat baking sheet or a cardboard round as support when lifting the layers. Assemble the tiers on cardboard rounds that are about ¼ inch smaller than the cakes themselves. Supports are inserted into the bottom tier so that the middle tier will rest directly on the larger base; the top tier has been elevated ½ inch, creating an airy look and allowing easy removal for the "anniversary" cake. If you make a mistake, just cover it with flowers. Or, if you prefer, decorate with buttercream roses and drop flowers.

EQUIPMENT

Two each 6-inch, 10-inch, and 14-inch round pans
6-, 10-, and 14-inch cardboard rounds
Ruler
8 chopsticks or drinking straws
36-inch wood skewer or ¼-inch dowel (optional)
Pruning scissors

Spray bottle
Ateco #5 and #8 round; #104 straight-edge; #67, #68, and #70 leaf tips
1 or 2 pastry bags
2 to 3 dozen fresh flowers
Fresh ivy, ferns, or other greens

WORK PLAN

Up to 2 days ahead—
Bake the Almond Genoise and prepare the Swiss Meringue Buttercream and Almond Buttercream filling.
Up to 1 day ahead—
Slice the strawberries and assemble and decorate the cake.
Baking & Preparation—
About 3½ hours
Assembly & Decoration—
About 3½ hours, including chilling time

RECIPE

4½ recipes Almond Genoise, Page 21

8 recipes Swiss Meringue Buttercream, Page 27

1 pound almond paste

2 cups heavy cream

2 pints strawberries

1½ cups Grand Marnier

PREPARATION

1. Mix and bake the cakes in stages, allowing 1½ recipes for the two 6-inch and two 10-inch layers, and 1½ recipes for each of the two 14-inch layers. Allow about 20 minutes' baking time for the 6-inch cakes, 25 for the 10-inch, and 40 for the 14-inch layers.

2. Make the buttercream in two batches of four recipes each. Set aside 1¼ batches—about 20 cups—for frosting and decoration. Keep the remaining 12 cups of buttercream at room temperature, to be flavored with almond cream and used to fill the cake. Repeat when necessary.

3. Place the almond paste in the large bowl of an electric mixer fitted with a paddle attachment if you have one. With the mixer at low speed, gradually add ¼ cup of heavy cream. Slowly beat in

the rest of the cream, then increase the speed until the mixture is fairly smooth. Because of the texture of the almond paste, the cream will not be completely smooth; do not overbeat it, or it may curdle. By hand, fold the almond cream into the 12 cups of buttercream. Return the bowl to the electric mixer and, using the whip attachment, mix at medium speed until well combined.

4. Cut the strawberries lengthwise into 3 or 4 slices each, and toss them with about ½ cup of Grand Marnier.

ASSEMBLY & DECORATION

5. Slice each layer of cake in half horizontally, using a long serrated knife. You will have twelve layers in all, four of each size.

6. Place a 14-inch layer on a slightly smaller cardboard round. Sprinkle with about ¼ cup of Grand Marnier and spread with about 2 cups of almond buttercream, using a metal spatula. Place the second 14-inch layer on top and cover with 2 cups of almond buttercream. Spread sliced strawberries over the almond buttercream. Position the third layer on top, sprinkle with Grand Marnier, and spread with about 2 cups of almond buttercream. Top with the fourth 14-inch layer and smooth any filling that may have seeped out between the layers. Refrigerate the cake until the filling is firm—15 to 30 minutes—or chill in the freezer for 5 to 10 minutes.

7. Assemble the 10-inch and 6-inch tiers in the same way, placing the bottom layer of each on a cardboard round. Sprinkle the 10-inch layers with 3 tablespoons of Grand Marnier, a layer of strawberries, and fill with about 1½ cups of buttercream; the 6-inch layers with about 1 tablespoon of Grand Marnier, strawberries, and about ½ cup of buttercream. Chill both tiers until the fillings are firm.

8. Cover the 14-inch tier with a thin layer of plain buttercream, beginning with the sides and ending with the top. Refrigerate until the frosting is firm—15 to 30 minutes. Meanwhile, frost the 10-inch and 6-inch tiers the same way, chilling each until the filling is firm.

9. Frost each tier again, more thickly this time, making sure the frosting is even and the edges of the cake are clearly defined. Chill the cakes again until the second layer of frosting is set and firm.

10. Frost the tiers a third time, finishing the buttercream with a spatula that has been warmed in hot water, then dried. Chill again until the frosting is firm. About 4 cups of buttercream will be left for piping the decorations.

11. Set the 14-inch tier, still on the cardboard round, on a serving platter. With pruning scissors, cut four lengths of chopsticks or plastic straws to the height of the tier, to use as supports for the second tier. Insert the supports into the cake about 5 inches apart at the corners of an imaginary square in the center of the cake. Or insert the supports in the cake and cut them flush with the top of the tier. Using a long metal spatula, carefully center the 10-inch tier, still on the cardboard round, on the supports in the bottom tier. Lightly spray the join with a little water and then smooth the buttercream around the base of the smaller tier, using a small, thin metal spatula, to conceal the join.

12. Measure the height of the 10-inch tier and cut four supports ½ inch higher than this measure. Insert these into the center of the 10-inch cake at the corners of an imaginary 3-inch square, with the extra ½ inch protruding. Center the 6-inch tier, still on the cardboard round, on top of the supports.

13. If you wish to anchor the tiers in place, follow the directions on page 150.

14. Begin the decoration of the cake with a #8 tip. Pipe a buttercream border around the base of the 6-inch tier, randomly interrupting the piping with small knots and flourishes. With the same tip, pipe similar borders around the top edges of the 10-inch and 14-inch tiers, curving the border slightly between the knots, again in random fashion to achieve an asymmetrical, free-flowing look. On the sides of the lower tiers, pipe curved swags diagonally from the edges of the top.

15. With a #5 tip, decorate the top tier in the same fashion.

16. Using a #104 tip, pipe a border around the base of the bottom tier, pressing out two knots about every 4 inches.

17. Using each of the three leaf tips in turn, pipe leaves of varying sizes onto the borders on each tier, including the bottom border, and onto the side decorations. Refrigerate to set the frosting.

18. Decorate the cake with fresh flowers just before serving. Begin with the large flowers on top of the cake. The stems may be wrapped in foil or set in straws inserted in the cake or pressed directly into the cake, as you prefer. Fill out the arrangement with smaller flowers and leaves. Set a second grouping on top of the bottom tier, if desired. Scatter more flowers on the lower tiers, gently pressing them into the buttercream. Arrange vines or ferns around the base.

Piping Free-Flowing Designs

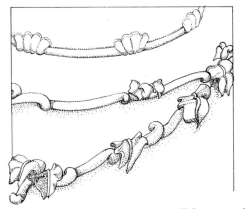

Use a #8 tip to pipe the random small knots and flourishes around the base of the 6-inch tier and the borders of the 10- and 14-inch tiers, as well as for the diagonal swags of the two larger tiers. A #5 tip decorates the borders and swags of the top tier and a #104 tip creates the border design of the base of the cake.

STORING & SERVING

The cake may be stored, uncovered, in the refrigerator for up to one day. In this case, the top tier should be removed first and stored on another shelf. Allow the cake to sit at room temperature for 1 to 3 hours before serving.

Before cutting the cake, remove the flowers and withdraw the anchor. With a metal spatula for support, lift off the 6-inch tier, which may be frozen as an anniversary cake: The 10-inch tier may be cut while it is in place, after removing the wood supports. After serving, lift off the cardboard round and cut the 14-inch tier.

GARLANDS OF FLOWERS WEDDING CAKE
·
Recipe, Page 157

CHOCOLATE NOCTURNE WEDDING CAKE

Photograph, Page 164
Chocolate Genoise filled with framboise, raspberry preserves, fresh raspberries, and Chocolate Whipped Cream; frosted with Ganache; and decorated with Chocolate Curls, Leaves, and Ribbons. Serves 50

Here is a good example of why chocolate wedding cakes are so popular today. Don't be daunted by the velvety-smooth chocolate perfection of the cake—think of it simply as three chocolate layer cakes, filled with fresh raspberries, raspberry preserves, framboise liqueur, and chocolate whipped cream.

Once you've filled the three cakes, stack them asymmetrically, as we have, for added drama, and coat them with a ganache so smooth it pours on and needs just a little help from a metal spatula to spread it to a satiny finish.

EQUIPMENT

Two baking sheets
18 fresh rose (or other) leaves
Pastry scraper
Two each 12-inch, 10-inch, 6-inch round pans
1 each 12-inch, 10-inch, and 6-inch cardboard rounds
Metal spatula
Foil or parchment paper
8 wood chopsticks or plastic straws
36-inch wood skewer or ¼-inch-thick dowel
Wire rack
Fine sieve or small strainer

WORK PLAN

Up to 4 days ahead—
Make the Chocolate Leaves, Curls, and Ribbons.
Up to 2 days ahead—
Bake the Chocolate Genoise.
Up to 1 day ahead—
Make the Chocolate Whipped Cream, assemble the cake, make the Ganache, and frost the cake.
Up to 4 hours ahead—
Decorate the cake with Leaves, Curls, and Ribbons.

Baking & Preparation—
About 4 hours
Assembly & Decoration—
About 2½ hours, including chilling time

RECIPE

18 ounces semisweet chocolate

4½ recipes Chocolate Genoise, Page 21

6 recipes Chocolate Whipped Cream, Page 29

1¼ cups framboise

1¾ cups raspberry preserves, strained

1½ pints fresh raspberries

4 recipes Ganache, Page 29

PREPARATION

1. Make the chocolate leaves, curls, and ribbons, following the instructions on page 70. Make about fifteen to twenty leaves, twenty to twenty-five curls, and eight to ten ribbons. Refrigerate until ready to decorate the cake.

2. Mix and bake the cakes in batches, allowing 1½ recipes for the 6- and 10-inch cakes, and 1½ recipes for each 12-inch cake. Test for doneness after 20 minutes for the 6-inch cake, 25 minutes for the 10-inch, and 30 minutes for the 12-inch.

3. Prepare the chocolate whipped cream.

ASSEMBLY & DECORATION

4. Using a long serrated knife, slice each layer in half horizontally. You will have twelve layers in all, four of each size.

5. Set one 12-inch layer on a slightly smaller cardboard round. Sprinkle with about 3½ tablespoons of framboise and lightly spread with about ½ cup of raspberry preserves. Using a metal spatula, generously spread the layer with about 2 cups of whipped cream. Place the second layer on top. Sprinkle this with framboise and spread with 2 cups of whipped cream. Cover the cream with a layer of fresh raspberries. Place the third layer on the raspberries, sprinkle with framboise, and

spread with 2 cups of whipped cream. Top with the remaining layer. Smooth any filling that may have seeped out the sides. Refrigerate the cake until the filling is set and firm—15 to 30 minutes—or chill it in the freezer—5 to 10 minutes.

6. Assemble the 10-inch and 6-inch cakes in the same way, setting the bottom layer of each on a slightly smaller cardboard round. Sprinkle the 10-inch layers with about 2 tablespoons of framboise and spread with about ¼ cup of preserves, 1½ cups of whipped cream, and raspberries. For the 6-inch layers, use 1 tablespoon of framboise, 2 tablespoons of preserves, raspberries, and ½ cup of cream. Refrigerate each cake as it is completed.

7. To support the second tier, use pruning scissors to cut 4 lengths of chopsticks or plastic straws to the height of the 12-inch cake. Insert the supports into the cake at the corners of an imaginary 5-inch square at one side of the top of the cake. Using a metal spatula, place the 10-inch cake, still on the cardboard round, on top of the larger cake so that it is supported by the chopsticks or straws. Cut 4 chopsticks or straws to the height of the 10-inch tier. Insert the supports at the corners of an imaginary 3-inch square at the same side of the top of the second tier. Set the 6-inch tier, on the cardboard round, on top of the supports.

8. If you prefer to anchor the tiers in place, follow the directions on page 150.

9. Line a baking sheet with foil or parchment paper and place a wire rack on the sheet. Transfer the assembled cake, still on the cardboard round, to the rack. Prepare the ganache. Pour the warm ganache over the cake and, starting from the top, use a metal spatula to smooth the top and sides of each tier and to encourage the ganache to run down and cover all three tiers.

10. Scrape up the ganache that has fallen onto the baking sheet and strain it back into the pan. Reheat it very slowly until the mixture regains a pouring consistency. Pour ganache over the cake again, smoothing it with a metal spatula. Scrape up the ganache from the baking sheet and strain it into the pan for attaching the curls and leaves to the cake. The cake should sit until the ganache sets, but is still slightly tacky.

11. Transfer the cake to a serving platter. Attach eight to ten tightly rolled curls to the top of the cake, arranging them to conceal the anchor and pressing them gently into the ganache. Group looser curls and ribbons in two or three spots on the bottom tiers, pressing them into the ganache. Finally, position the leaves on the cake, setting them behind and against the curls and ribbons. Use extra ganache to hold the curls and leaves in place.

Stacking "Step" Tiers

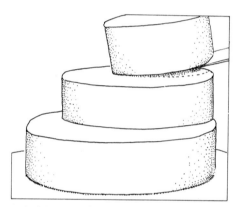

Use a toothpick to outline on the lowest tier exactly where the middle tier should be placed. Next, using a spatula or cardboard round and steadying the cake with your hand, place it gently onto the outlined area. Repeat with the top tier. The entire cake should form a "step" with one side flush, creating a straight vertical line.

STORING & SERVING

Without the curls and leaves, the frosted cake may be kept in the refrigerator, uncovered, for up to 1 day. Allow the cake to sit at room temperature for at least 30 minutes before decorating it with curls and leaves.

To serve the cake, remove the curls from the top tier, then withdraw the anchor. Cut the top tier into servings, or use a metal spatula to lift it off and set aside for a first anniversary. Cut the 10-inch layer while it is still in place, after removing the supports. When it has been served, lift off its cardboard round and cut the largest tier.

CHOCOLATE NOCTURNE WEDDING CAKE
·
Recipe, Page 161

PRETTY CAKES

PORCELAIN ROSE CAKE

Photograph, Page 168
Lemon Genoise filled with apricot preserves and Lemon Buttercream, frosted with Lemon Buttercream and covered with Rolled Fondant and decorated with a fondant rose. Serves 8 to 10

For an intimate wedding, engagement, or anniversary celebration, this light lemon genoise is filled with apricot preserves and lemon buttercream, then draped with pure white rolled fondant. At a glance, the cake looks as smooth and perfect as fine white china.

The central rose is rolled fondant, cut and shaped into petals, then assembled. The rose and leaves are made with the same techniques as those described for marzipan roses and leaves, but the fondant will dry out even more quickly than marzipan and should be kept covered as much as possible. The rose and leaves are fixed to the cake with a drop of water brushed on their bases, but care is necessary as water can stain the fondant.

If you prefer, a recipe of fruitcake can replace the genoise. In this case, omit the buttercream, trim the top of the cake to make it flat, and invert it on a cardboard round. Spread ⅔ cup of strained apricot preserves over the sides and top of the cake, then cover with fondant. This moist, rich cake is particularly suitable for a noteworthy anniversary.

The fondant will keep the cake fresh, and as fondant needs a couple of days at room temperature to dry out, this is definitely a cake you can make well ahead of time. A slender ecru satin ribbon around the base completes the simple but effective decoration.

EQUIPMENT

6-inch pan, 4 inches deep
Cardboard round
Rolling pin
Leaf cutter and press
Parchment paper
Petal cutter or large decorating tip
Small paintbrush
1½ yards ecru satin ribbon, ¼ inch wide

WORK PLAN

Up to 5 days ahead—
Bake the Lemon Genoise, and prepare the Lemon Buttercream, Rolled Fondant, and fondant rose with leaves. Assemble cake, frost, cover with Fondant and decorate.
Baking & Preparation—
About 2 hours
Assembly & Decoration—
About 1½ hours

RECIPE

½ recipe Lemon Genoise, *Page 21*

½ recipe Lemon Buttercream, *Page 28*

1 recipe Rolled Fondant, *Page 33*

⅔ cup strained apricot preserves

½ cup confectioners' sugar or cornstarch

PREPARATION

1. Bake the genoise in a 6-inch round pan. Prepare the buttercream and the rolled fondant.

ASSEMBLY & DECORATION

2. Set the cake on a flat surface. With a long serrated knife, slice the cake horizontally into three even layers.

3. Place the bottom layer on a cardboard round. Using a metal spatula, spread the cake with ⅓ cup preserves and ⅓ cup buttercream. Place the second layer over the cream and spread with the same amount of preserves and buttercream. Position the third layer on top and smooth any filling that may have seeped out the sides. Refrigerate the cake until the filling has set—15 to 25 minutes.

4. Spread a thin layer of buttercream over the cake, beginning with the sides and ending with the top. As fondant will cover the frosting, the buttercream need not be finely finished. Do not refrigerate the cake.

5. Reserve 4 ounces of fondant for the rose and leaves. Sprinkle a work surface with a little confectioners' sugar or cornstarch and roll the fondant to a 14-inch circle about ⅛ inch thick.

Following the general directions for working with marzipan on page 77, center and drape the fondant over the cake. Dust your hands with sugar or cornstarch and gently pat the fondant into place, smoothing the folds and creases. Trim the excess fondant with a paring knife. Set the cake aside.

6. Sprinkle the work surface with sugar or cornstarch and roll out the reserved fondant to a thickness of ⅛ inch. Cut two leaves of fondant and mold them in the leaf press, following the directions on page 147. Twist the shaped leaves and set aside on parchment paper. With a petal cutter or large decorating tip, cut the petals and assemble the rose, following the illustrated instructions on page 74.

7. With a small paintbrush, very lightly moisten the bottom of the rose with water. Gently press the rose into the center of the cake. Moisten and attach the leaves on one side of the rose.

8. Transfer the cake to a serving plate. Tie the longer ribbon around the base of the cake in a long bow. Tie the second ribbon into a double bow and attach it to the first bow, securing it by looping the longer bow over it.

STORING & SERVING

Store the cake at room temperature for 1 or 2 days to allow the fondant to dry. The fondant acts as a seal, keeping the cake underneath fresh and moist. In fact, the cake can be kept under a cake dome for up to 5 days.

CAMEO WEDDING CAKE

Photograph, Page 169
Alternating layers of Genoise and Chocolate Genoise,
flavored with kirsch, filled and frosted with White
Chocolate Buttercream, covered with Rolled Fondant,
and decorated with Royal Icing. Serves 30 to 35

Delicate and elegant, this cake has the look of lacy white flowers embroidered on creamy satin, achieved by outlining flowers with bright white royal icing on a background of tinted rolled fondant. You may copy the pattern in the photograph or create your own: This one was inspired by a pair of curtains. Exquisite bridal lace, from this wedding or one of years past, will convey a special significance. You may want to rough out the design on paper first, to copy as you pipe the icing onto the cake. For texture, the outline is sometimes filled in, and overpiped for height. If you make a mistake in the piping, simply chip it off gently, using a spatula or small knife.

Beneath the fondant, alternating layers of genoise and chocolate genoise are brushed with a kirsch-flavored syrup and filled with white chocolate buttercream. The cake needs to be made at least two days ahead to allow the fondant to dry; once it's been covered, it will stay fresh for several days.

EQUIPMENT

One to four 11½- by 15½-inch jelly roll pans
Parchment paper
14-inch cardboard round
Pastry brush
Ateco #2 and #4 round tips
One or two pastry bags

WORK PLAN

Up to 5 days ahead—
Bake the Genoise and Chocolate Genoise, and prepare the White Chocolate Buttercream, Stock Syrup, Rolled Fondant, and Royal Icing; assemble and cover the cake with fondant.
At least 2 hours ahead—
Decorate the cake with Royal Icing.
Baking & Preparation—
About 3½ hours

Assembly & Decoration—
About 3 hours

RECIPE

2 recipes Genoise, Page 20

2 recipes Chocolate Genoise, Page 21

1½ recipes White Chocolate Buttercream, Page 28

6 tablespoons Stock Syrup, Page 34

2 recipes Rolled Fondant, Page 33

1 recipe Royal Icing, Page 30

6 tablespoons kirsch

Yellow and brown paste food coloring

½ cup confectioners' sugar or cornstarch

PREPARATION

1. Bake the genoises in 11½- by 15½-inch jelly roll pans, one recipe per pan.

2. Prepare the buttercream, stock syrup, rolled fondant, and royal icing. Mix together the stock syrup and kirsch.

3. Cut an oval template 14 inches long and 10 inches wide, from parchment paper. Trim a cardboard round to this same size.

ASSEMBLY & DECORATION

4. When the cakes have cooled, trim each to the shape of the oval template, using a long serrated knife.

5. Place a layer of chocolate genoise on the cardboard oval. Brush the cake with ¼ cup of the kirsch syrup. Using a metal spatula, spread 1½ cups of buttercream over the cake. Position a layer of genoise over the buttercream. Brush with syrup and spread with buttercream. Top with another chocolate genoise. Brush with syrup and spread with buttercream. Place the final genoise layer over the buttercream. Smooth any filling that may have seeped out the sides, and refrigerate the cake until the filling is firm—20 to 30 minutes.

PORCELAIN ROSE CAKE
·
Recipe, Page 165

CAMEO WEDDING CAKE
·
Recipe, Page 167

6. Using a long serrated knife, bevel the top edge of the cake so that the sides are rounded and smooth.

7. Frost the cake with 1½ cups of buttercream, beginning with the sides and ending with the top. As the frosting will be completely concealed under the fondant, the buttercream need not be finely finished. Do not refrigerate the cake.

8. Tint the fondant a deep cream color, using yellow food coloring mixed with a tiny amount of brown.

9. Sprinkle a work surface with confectioners' sugar or cornstarch. Roll out the fondant to a 22-inch oval about ⅛ inch thick. Center and drape the fondant over the cake, following the directions on page 77. Gently pat the fondant into place, smoothing any creases and folds. Trim the excess fondant from the base of the cake with a paring knife. Allow the cake to sit at room temperature for one to two days to dry the fondant before adding the decoration.

10. Transfer the cake to a serving platter. With a toothpick, faintly outline the pattern on the rolled fondant. Fit a pastry bag with a #2 tip and partially fill with royal icing. Beginning at the center, pipe over the outline. Use light, decreasing pressure for the wisps and medium pressure for flowers. Fill in the centers of flowers and leaves with small dots.

11. Thin ½ cup of the remaining icing with 3 drops of water. Spoon this mixture into a clean pastry bag fitted with the #2 tip. Pipe over the borders of the flowers; allow the icing to dry, and pipe over again.

12. Fit a pastry bag with a #4 tip and partially fill with undiluted royal icing. Pipe a bead border around the base of the cake, spacing the beads so that they do not touch.

Piping Embossed Designs

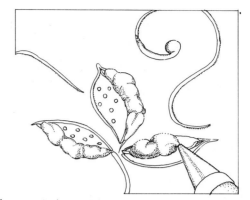

Using a #2 tip, position the bag directly over the pattern. Pipe in the outline and allow to dry. Pipe over the first layer, again allow to dry, and pipe over a third time.

STORING & SERVING

Once it has been covered with fondant, the cake should not be refrigerated, but may be stored at room temperature, loosely covered or under a cake dome, for 1 to 2 days.

CAMELLIA SHOWER CAKE

Photograph, Page 172
Genoise flavored with framboise, filled with raspberry
preserves and Framboise Buttercream, frosted with
Framboise Buttercream, covered with marzipan, and
decorated with Pastillage flowers and Royal Icing.
Serves 18 to 24

Breathtakingly beautiful, this cake epitomizes the art of cake decorating. The graceful bevel underscores two distinctive design elements—hundreds of tiny, precisely piped icing beads that surround a bouquet of extraordinary pastillage flowers. Pastillage, a time-honored decorating material, is a paste rolled out to exquisite thinness, then cut and shaped into petals. When dry, the result is a beautiful, bisquelike finish. Pastillage takes food coloring wonderfully, both mixed in before shaping and painted on afterward.

When shaping the petals, work quickly as pastillage stiffens in just a few minutes. Always keep the pastillage you are not working on covered. When the petals have dried for at least a day, they are assembled with royal icing and allowed to dry for another day. Pastillage is extremely brittle and fragile, so do make extra petals, and make the flowers at least several days ahead. Here the flowers are finished with pearl-tipped stamens, which can be purchased at card shops.

EQUIPMENT

Two 12-inch round pans
One 12-inch cardboard round
Turntable
Ateco #1 or 2 and 3 round, #65 and #70 leaf, #101 rose tips
Pastry bag
Parchment paper
2- and 1½-inch teardrop cutters
2 yards of ½-inch white satin ribbon
½ yard of ½-inch pink satin ribbon
Sixteen to twenty pearl-tipped stamens
Two parchment paper piping cones
Rolling pin

WORK PLAN

Up to 1 week ahead—
Make the Pastillage flowers.
Up to 2 days ahead—
Bake the Genoise, make the Framboise Buttercream

and the Royal Icing. Assemble the cake, frost, and cover with marzipan.
At least 2 hours ahead—
Decorate with Pastillage flowers and Royal Icing.
Baking & Preparation—
About 2 hours
Assembly & Decoration—
About 3 hours, including chilling time

RECIPE

1 recipe Pastillage, Page 35

Red (or pink), brown, and green food coloring

1 cup cornstarch

½ cup confectioners' sugar

2 recipes Royal Icing, Page 30

1½ recipes Genoise, Page 20

1 recipe Framboise Buttercream, Page 28

¼ cup Stock Syrup, Page 34

¼ cup framboise

½ cup seedless raspberry preserves

14 ounces marzipan

PREPARATION

1. Prepare the pastillage for the flowers at least two days ahead. With red and a tiny amount of brown food coloring (or pink coloring), tint the pastillage to a warm pink. To cut the pastillage flower petals, sprinkle a work surface with cornstarch and cut petals with a teardrop cutter. To keep the icing and petals pliable until they have been cut and shaped, cover them with plastic and a damp cloth. Cut one petal at a time and put each back under the plastic and cloth to prevent drying out.

2. Dust the palms of your hands with cornstarch. Remove a petal from the plastic wrap and, holding it in one hand, feather and thin the edges with the tips of the thumb and forefinger of your other hand so that it resembles the petals in the photograph. Cup the petal in one palm and with the fingertip of the other hand, press in the center to curl petal slightly. Transfer the petal to foam

CAMELLIA SHOWER CAKE
·
Recipe, Page 171

PRETTY CAKES

rubber or several kitchen towels to dry. Repeat with all the petals. Allow them to dry at room temperature for 24 hours.

3. When the petals have dried, make the royal icing and tint ¼ cup to match the pastillage. (Store the remaining icing in an airtight container.) Form a flower using the icing as a glue. Repeat for the second flower. Make the larger center blossom in the same way, but incorporate an extra tier in the center and a larger base. Return the blossoms to the foam rubber or towel to dry for at least 3 hours. Pipe centers of pink icing into each flower. Insert five stamens in the center of each small flower and seven in the larger.

4. Bake the genoise in two 12-inch round pans. Prepare the buttercream. Make the stock syrup and mix with the framboise.

ASSEMBLY & DECORATION

5. When the cake has cooled, place a bottom layer on a cardboard round. Brush the cake with the framboise syrup and spread with raspberry preserves. Using a metal spatula, spread about ¾ cup of buttercream over the preserves. Top with the second layer, and smooth any filling that may have seeped out the sides. Refrigerate the cake until the filling is firm—15 to 30 minutes.

6. Place the cake on a turntable. With a long serrated knife, bevel the top edge to a smoothly rounded finish.

7. Seal the cake with a thin layer of buttercream. Keep the cake at room temperature.

8. Sprinkle a work surface with confectioners' sugar. Roll the marzipan to a 16-inch circle about ⅛ inch thick. Center and drape the marzipan over the cake. With your hand palm-side down, smooth marzipan in a circular motion over the top of the cake. Gently mold the marzipan to the sides of the cake. Trim the excess from the base with a paring knife. Do not refrigerate the cake. Allow marzipan to dry for at least 6 hours for a smooth decorating surface.

9. With the cake on the turntable, measure the circumference of the cake. Divide this figure by 8 to determine the length of the wavelike arcs around the side. Cut a parchment template to this measure and shape. Using a toothpick, lightly trace the template around the side of the cake. Alternatively, you may draw the arcs on the cake with a thin thread of piped royal icing; after the icing hardens, gently scrape it off the cake and follow the faint line it leaves to pipe the tiny dots.

10. Half-fill a pastry bag with royal icing and fit the bag with a #1 or 2 tip, or fill a parchment cone and cut a tiny opening. The icing should be slightly thinned with one or two drops of water before being put in the pastry bag. Pipe tiny dots along the outlined arcs, as small and close together as possible.

11. Starting at the center of the cake, pipe slightly larger dots around the entire cake about ⅛ inch apart. Slowly rotate the turntable and hold the bag in the same place, squeezing it in a steady rhythm so the dots are even. Hold the bag so the tip barely skims the surface of the marzipan, and alternate the pressure so that the icing is released in spurts (not in a steady flow, which would create a line). In the end, the dots actually spiral to the outside edge of the cake, although the effect is one of perfect rows.

12. Tint ½ cup of royal icing to match the pastillage flowers. Spoon the icing into a pastry bag fitted with a #3 tip or parchment cone with small opening. Pipe three dabs of icing on top of the cake, one where each blossom will go. Carefully set the pastillage flowers on the icing, moving them with a small spatula.

13. Tint 1 cup of royal icing a soft mint green. Fit a pastry bag with a #70 tip and half-fill it with green icing. Pipe leaves around the blossoms, moving the bag with a slight up-and-down motion to create a rippled, curled look. Pipe three leaves on each of the smaller blossoms and seven on the central flower.

14. Fit a pastry bag with a #101 tip and partially fill with pink icing. Pipe tiny buds around the side

of the cake at the base of each arc. Spoon green icing into a pastry bag fitted with a #65 tip. Pipe one or two leaves under each bud.

Making Pastillage Flowers

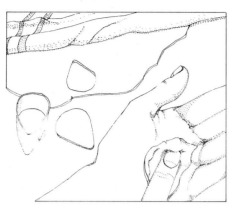

Sprinkle work surface with cornstarch and roll out 1 cup of tinted pastillage to ¹⁄₁₆ to ⅛ inch thickness. With teardrop cutters, cut out about ten 2-inch petals and twenty-five 1½-inch petals. Additionally, cut the tops off 6 of the 1½-inch petals, so they are about ¾-inch long, to be used for central flower. Dust palms with cornstarch and crimp the edges of the petals.

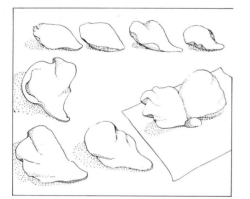

After allowing to dry, arrange and overlap petals to form a flower.

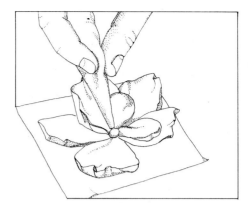

Using a pastry bag fitted with a #1 tip, pipe icing (tinted to match flowers) into the center of the flower to hold petals together. It is helpful to form the flowers on squares of waxed or parchment paper.

When petals have been arranged in tiers, with five 2-inch petals on the outside and four 1½-inch petals on the inside, insert store-bought stamens into the center, allow to dry and delicately place flower on cake. The center flower takes six 2-inch petals as the base, four 1½-inch petals as the second tier, and three ¾-inch petals for the center.

STORING & SERVING

Transfer the cake to a serving platter. Cut ½ yard of white ribbon and set aside. Wrap 1½ yards of white ribbon around the base of the cake, tying it in a bow. Holding ½ yard each of pink and white ribbon together, tie them into a bow. Place this bow over the bow on the cake, securing it in place with the ribbon ends of the first bow, or with a straight pin concealed within the center. Remove the ribbons, pastillage flowers, and straight pin before cutting the cake.

HEIRLOOM WEDDING CAKE
Recipe, Page 177

HEIRLOOM WEDDING CAKE

Photograph, Page 176
Orange Genoise brushed with Grand Marnier syrup,
filled and frosted with Orange Buttercream, covered
with Marzipan, and decorated with Pastillage and
Royal Icing flowers and sugar bells. Serves 40 to 60

Orange blossoms are a bridal tradition, and the unconventional shape of this cake gives them a refreshingly modern feeling. Delicately shaped from pastillage, the flowers are subtly tinted after drying. Royal icing drop flowers, lilies of the valley, and sugar bells are set off by satin bows and tulle net. The marzipan covering the cake adds a velvety texture, enhanced by crimping its edges.

The lilies of the valley are made with pastillage, shaped and then inserted individually onto wire. The sugar bells are molded from sugar dampened with egg white, and attached to the satin and tulle bows. (To save time, both the flowers and the bells can be purchased at card and party shops and bakers' supply houses.)

Crimping is the term for the unusual finish along the edges of the cake. Crimpers are available from H. France Company (see Sources of Supply, page 188), and the technique is very much like finishing a pie crust. However, if you do not have one, the cake is equally lovely without this effect.

EQUIPMENT

One to three 11½- by 15½-inch jelly roll pans
Rolling pin
1½-inch teardrop cutter
12-inch-square piece of foam rubber, or folded kitchen towels
Small paintbrush
Cardboard round
Crimping tool
Ateco #1 round and #131 flower tips
Pastry bag
Sixteen white or pearl-tipped stamens
Twelve silver stamens
Tweezers (optional)
4 yards white satin ribbon, ¼-inch wide
Parchment paper
Two 7-inch by 11-inch pieces of white tulle
50 inches white wire

WORK PLAN

Up to 2 weeks ahead—
Make Pastillage flowers, Royal Icing drop flowers, sugar bells, lilies of the valley, ribbons, and bows.
Up to 2 days ahead—
Bake the cakes and prepare the buttercream and stock syrup; assemble and cover the cake with marzipan.
Baking & Preparation—
About 5 hours, plus drying time
Assembly & Decoration—
About 2½ hours, including chilling time

RECIPE

½ cup cornstarch

½ cup confectioners' sugar

1 recipe Pastillage, Page 35

1 cup Royal Icing, Page 30

Yellow paste food coloring

1¼ cups granulated sugar

3 recipes Orange Genoise, Page 21

2 recipes Orange Buttercream, Page 28

35 ounces marzipan

1 egg white

½ cup Stock Syrup, Page 34

½ cup Grand Marnier

PREPARATION

1. The pastillage and royal icing flowers and bells need drying time and so should be made at least 2 days ahead. Make the pastillage and royal icing. Keep both in airtight containers.

2. For the pastillage blossoms, sprinkle a work surface with confectioners' sugar and roll out one-quarter of the pastillage to about ⅛ inch thickness. Using the teardrop cutter, cut out as many petals as you can. Work quickly and cover the petals with plastic and a damp cloth as soon as they are cut to prevent hardening. Continue rolling out the pastillage in batches until you have twenty-five to thirty petals.

3. Dust the palm of one hand with confectioners' sugar. Holding a petal in one hand, feather and thin the edges with the tips of the thumb and forefinger of your other hand, shaping the pastillage to simulate flower petals. Cup the petal in one palm and with the fingertip of your other hand, press in the center to curl petal slightly. Set the petal to dry on foam rubber or kitchen towels, and repeat with each of the remaining petals. Allow the petals to dry.

4. Tint ¼ cup of royal icing to pale yellow. Spoon the yellow icing into a pastry bag fitted with a #1 tip or a parchment cone with a small opening. Form the dried petals into four flowers, five petals to each, fixing their centers with royal icing. (For illustrated directions on pastillage flowers, see page 174.)

5. Pipe a dot of tinted icing in the center of each flower and insert four to five stamens in each. Return the flowers to the foam rubber or towel and allow to dry again for about 3 hours.

6. With untinted royal icing, pipe thirty-five to forty drop flowers, using a #131 tip. Pipe the flowers directly onto parchment. Let these dry overnight.

7. With the same untinted royal icing, pipe a center dot into each flower. Let dry 1 hour.

8. Dilute the yellow coloring with water. Dip the tip of a small paintbrush into the coloring and then shake off as much liquid as possible. Lightly paint the uppermost edges of the petals and the inside center of each flower.

9. Lightly paint the center and top edges of the drop flowers.

10. To make the 4 sugar bells, place one cup of granulated sugar in a large bowl and add 1 teaspoon of unbeaten egg white. With your hands mix the sugar with the egg white until the mixture stays compressed in your palms. Continue to add 1 teaspoon of egg white at a time until the mixture reaches this desired consistency. Follow the illustrated instructions for molding each bell in a bell mold and attaching stamens (see Sources of Supply for availability) and dry the bell at least 24 hours, preferably longer. Place the bell on the cake and attach it with royal icing. Sugar bells can be kept in airtight containers up to one year, so it's always a good idea to have extra on hand in case of breakage.

11. For the lilies of the valley, roll pastillage balls between palms dusted with confectioners' sugar and push the end of a paintbrush handle into the center of the ball to make a cup. Let dry a few minutes.

12. Cut 8 lengths of wire, varying their length between 3 and 5 inches. Curve the wires with your fingers and twist them around each other to make short twigs. Attach lilies of the valley to the wires, gluing them with royal icing. Let dry overnight. You may need to use tweezers and you will need a steady hand.

13. Bake the cakes in jelly roll pans and prepare the buttercream. Prepare the stock syrup and mix with the Grand Marnier.

ASSEMBLY & DECORATION

14. When the cakes have cooled, trim ¼ to ½ inch from each edge. Cut a cardboard to this size and set one layer on the cardboard. Brush the cake with Grand Marnier syrup and spread with 1½ to 2 cups of buttercream, using a metal spatula. Place the second layer on top; brush with syrup and spread with buttercream. Top with the third layer, and smooth any filling that may have seeped out between the layers. Refrigerate the cake until the filling is firm—15 to 30 minutes.

15. Spread a thin layer of buttercream over the sides and top of the cake to seal. Do not refrigerate.

16. Sprinkle a work surface with confectioners' sugar. Roll out the marzipan to a 15- by 19-inch rectangle. Center and drape the marzipan over the cake. Smooth and pat the marzipan into place, easing out any folds or wrinkles. Trim the excess from the base with a paring knife.

17. Crimp the top edges of the marzipan all around the cake, using a crimping tool. Crimp the base edge of the cake as well. If the marzipan is allowed to harden for a few hours or overnight, the

cake will be easier to decorate. Keep the cake at room temperature until ready to decorate.

18.   Thin ½ cup of royal icing with ¼ teaspoon of water. Spoon into a pastry bag with a #1 tip, and pipe curlicues and flourishes at each corner of the cake. Pipe tiny dots between the backs of the curlicues and at the edges of the top. Reserve some icing to pipe dots around the drop flowers added to the center of the cake.

19.   Attach pastillage blossoms.

20.   Attach the drop flowers around the pastillage blossoms, setting each in a dab of royal icing piped onto the cake and arranging them in clusters of four and five. Set more flowers in two diagonally opposite corners of the cake, in slightly larger groups of nine or ten flowers, centering them above the flourishes.

21.   Using the thinned royal icing, pipe short rows of tiny dots around the flowers in the center of the cake.

22.   With dabs of unthinned royal icing, attach the sugar bells to the cake in two diagonal corners.

23.   Insert the lilies of the valley on wires into the corners and center of the cake decorated with drop flowers.

24.   To make the center bow, cut a yard length of ribbon and bend it to form a six-loop bow about 6 inches across. Anchor the center by wrapping it two or three times with wire, leaving a 1½-inch length of wire to insert into the cake.

25.   To make the corner bows, cut two 24-inch lengths of ribbon and form them into two smaller, six-loop bows about 3 inches across. Gather one 7-inch by 11-inch piece of tulle in the center into loose folds. Wrap the tulle and a bow together in the center with wire to anchor into the cake. Repeat for second tulle bow.

26.   Insert the tulle and satin bows into the undecorated corners of the cake.

27.   Transfer the cake to a serving platter. Wrap the sides of the cake with satin ribbon, tying a small bow at the front. Trim the ribbon ends.

Piping Drop Flowers

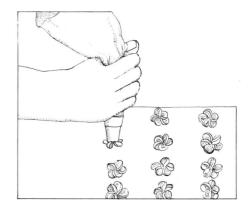

Partially fill the pastry bag with royal icing, and fit with a #131 tip. Holding the bag upright over parchment paper pivot your hand as far to the left as you can. Touch the tip to the paper and exert medium pressure, while turning your hand to the right. Stop squeezing and lift the bag straight up. Repeat for thirty-five to forty flowers.

Making Sugar Bells

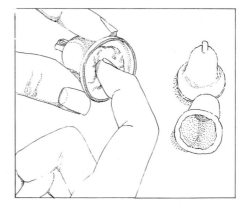

Press the moistened sugar tightly into a bell mold and level it off across the open end with a knife. Let the bell dry in the mold for 15 to 30 minutes. Use a paring knife or toothpick to hollow out the bell, leaving about ⅛-inch shell. Gently release the bell onto wax paper, and dry for 24 hours before attaching a pearl-tipped stamen with a dab of royal icing. Repeat for each bell.

Creating Lilies of the Valley

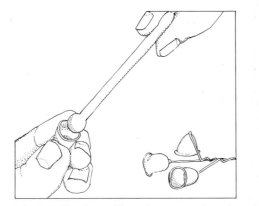

Roll ¼-inch balls of pastillage between palms dusted with confectioners' sugar. Holding each ball gently, push the end of a small paintbrush handle into the center to make a cup. Intertwine cups with stems formed from wires, glued with icing. Make six to ten lily bells per stem, making a total of about ten stems. Set each to dry on foam rubber or folded kitchen towels for 24 hours.

Crimping Marzipan

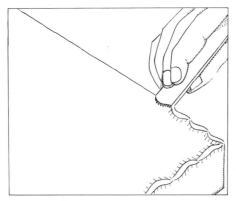

Starting at one corner of the cake, pinch the crimper together to crimp the edges of the marzipan. Repeat for the base, holding the crimper perpendicular to the side of the cake.

STORING & SERVING

The decorated cake may be kept at room temperature overnight, as the marzipan will keep the cake fresh. (Do not refrigerate a marzipan-covered cake, or the marzipan will become tacky.) To serve, remove the bows, sugar bells, lilies of the valley, and pastillage flowers. Cut the cake into rectangular slices.

THE LOHENGRIN

Recipe, Page 182

THE LOHENGRIN

Photograph, Page 181
An anniversary tier of fruitcake sprinkled with
Frangelico-flavored syrup, filled with apricot jam, sealed
with Buttercream, covered with Marzipan and
Poured Fondant, and decorated with Royal Icing,
marzipan flowers, and fresh flowers; three tiers of
Chocolate Genoise, brushed with Frangelico-flavored
syrup, filled with Swiss Meringue Buttercream, covered
with fondant, and decorated with Royal Icing and
marzipan and fresh flowers. Serves 100

This elegant, spectacular centerpiece is designed for a grand reception. Each tier has been gracefully beveled and gilded with shimmering poured fondant. The daintiest, most delicate marzipan flowers are set on the sides, framed with tiny royal icing dots and slim bands of satin ribbon circle the top tiers. Peruvian lilies, creamy white freesias, and baby's breath adorn the top tiers.

The top tier itself is fruitcake filled with apricot jam, especially suitable as an anniversary cake. The lower tiers are chocolate genoise, brushed with a Frangelico syrup and filled with buttercream. Once beveled, the tiers are covered with marzipan, then glazed with fondant.

Poured fondant can be tricky to work with and if you haven't used it before, we recommend making a "practice" tier several weeks in advance. Beyond the technique of pouring fondant and the sheer size of the cake, this recipe is not so demanding as it may seem. The decorative pattern is repeated on each tier.

The tiers can be decorated well in advance and put together with the separators, which are available at bakers' supply stores. (For more information on separators, see page 152.) Alternatively, the tiers can be assembled without the separators, directly on top of each other for a more compact but still dramatic cake.

When the tiers have been filled and coated with fondant, the supporting dowels are assembled to ensure a clean fit. The cake is then taken apart so that the tiers can be decorated and then reassembled. Supporting the cake, and acting as the platter, is a round flakeboard purchased at a lumberyard; this in turn rests on four flakeboard cubes that are glued underneath it.

Finally, the fresh flowers on each tier should be kept in cold water until an hour or so before being added to the cake. The larger stems are slipped into lengths of plastic straws that have been inserted into the cake; the others are pushed directly into the cake. Nearly any variety of nontoxic flowers can be used, whatever is seasonal. Baby's breath is an enchanting filler, and shiny dark leaves add vibrancy to the cake.

EQUIPMENT

Rolling pin
Kemper tool #PC5R 1/16-inch cutter
One small paintbrush
Two 3-foot square sheets thin foam rubber or several folded kitchen towels
One 18-inch round flakeboard, 3/4 to 1 inch thick
Four 2-inch flakeboard cubes
Wood and plastic glue
One 6-inch round pan, 3 inches deep
One or two each 8-, 10-, and 14-inch round pans
One each 6-, 8-, 10-, and two 14-inch cardboard rounds, taped together
Double boiler
Candy thermometer, with gradation below 100°F
Five wire racks
Five shallow pans
One 10-inch flat-top plastic separator, with four dowels
Two 8-inch plastic separators, with four dowels and four 5-inch columns
Two 6-inch plastic separators, with four dowels and four 5-inch columns
One ruler
One heavy-duty turntable
Ateco #1 round and #3 star tips
Two to three ounces marzipan, or two 2- to 3-inch cubes florists' styrofoam

WORK PLAN

Up to 2 weeks ahead—
Make about 200 marzipan flowers.
Up to 2 days ahead—
Bake the Chocolate Genoise and Fruitcake. Prepare the Amaretto and Swiss Meringue Buttercreams, Stock Syrup, and the Royal Icing. Assemble the cakes and cover with marzipan.
Baking & Preparation—
About 4 hours
Assembly & Decoration—
About 6 to 10 hours, including chilling time

RECIPE

9 pounds marzipan

Lavender food coloring

2 cups confectioners' sugar

1 recipe Fruitcake, Page 25

¾ cup apricot jam

5½ recipes Chocolate Genoise, Page 21

¾ cup Frangelico

½ cup Stock Syrup, Page 34

3 recipes Swiss Meringue Buttercream, Page 27

6 pounds fondant

3 recipes Royal Icing, Page 30

2 bunches baby's breath, 3 dozen cut flowers

PREPARATION

1. Make the marzipan flowers in batches. Tint about 2 pounds of marzipan to a very pale lavender. Divide this into four batches. Keep the remainder in a covered container and roll out the first batch as thinly as possible on a work surface sprinkled with confectioners' sugar. Working as quickly as possible, cut out about ten flowers with the Kemper tool. Cover the remaining rolled-out marzipan.

2. Transfer the flowers to a sheet of foam rubber or folded kitchen towels. With the tip of a small paintbrush handle, press gently but firmly into the center of each flower to curl the petals. Repeat the process with the remaining rolled-out marzipan, and then with the remaining three batches. Because the marzipan begins to stiffen almost as soon as it's exposed to air, you must work in small batches at a quick pace. Set the flowers aside to dry at room temperature for at least 24 hours.

3. To prepare the round flakeboard base and supports for the cake, measure the diameter of your turntable. Mark a square on the underside of the flakeboard base that will allow clearance of the cubes when they have been glued to the base, but make sure they do not show under the flake-board round. Glue the cubes to the bottom of the base and allow several hours of drying time.

4. Mix and bake the fruitcake in a 6-inch round pan. When it is cool, slice it in half horizontally and spread with ½ cup apricot jam. Place the second layer on top and set aside.

5. Bake the genoise in batches according to your mixer and oven capacity, allowing 1½ recipes for each 14-inch pan, 1½ recipes to divide between the 10-inch pans, and 1 recipe to divide between the 8-inch pans. Make two layers of each size. Prepare the buttercream.

6. To assemble the cakes, combine the Frangelico and stock syrup. Place one layer on a cardboard round; brush with the syrup, spread with buttercream, and top with the second layer. Allow ¼ cup syrup and 2 cups buttercream for the 14-inch; 3 tablespoons syrup and 1½ cups buttercream for the 10-inch; and 2 tablespoons syrup and ¾ cup buttercream for the 8-inch layers. Smooth any filling that may have seeped out the layers, and refrigerate to set the filling—15 to 30 minutes.

7. Bevel the top layer of each tier, including the fruitcake. Spread the remaining apricot jam over the fruitcake to form a thin coating. Seal each of the genoise tiers with a thin coating of buttercream. Also, spread a thin layer of buttercream over the top and sides of the flakeboard base.

8. Sprinkle a work surface with confectioners' sugar. Roll out 28 ounces of marzipan to a 20-inch circle, ⅛ to ¼ inch thick. Center and drape the marzipan over the flakeboard base, smoothing the marzipan and patting out any creases or wrinkles. Trim the excess from the bottom with a paring knife.

9. Sprinkle the work surface with more sugar and roll out 28 ounces of marzipan to a 20-inch circle. Drape this over the 14-inch tier, smoothing it evenly over the cake.

10. Cover the three remaining tiers. For the 10-inch tier, roll 21 ounces of marzipan to a 16-inch circle; 18 ounces to a 14-inch circle for the 8-inch tier; and 16 ounces to a 12-inch circle for the 6-inch fruitcake.

11. Place the marzipan-covered flakeboard on a wire rack set over a shallow pan.

12. Place half the fondant in the top of a double boiler set over hot—not boiling—water. With a wooden spoon, stir the fondant up from the bottom of the pan as it melts. Set a candy thermometer in the pot and heat the fondant to between 90° and 95°F. Feel the fondant with the back of your index finger; it should be no warmer than body temperature.

13. Stir 2 to 3 tablespoons of hot water into the fondant to thin it to a pouring consistency. When it's ready to pour, the fondant will coat the back of a wooden spoon and when lifted on the spoon and then dropped back, the ribbon of fondant will disappear after a second or two. Remove the top of the double boiler and dry the bottom with a kitchen towel. Holding the pan about 6 inches over the board, pour the fondant onto the center of the board. With a metal spatula, spread it across the top so that it falls down to cover the sides. Spread the fondant to fill in any uncovered areas, applying a thin layer but one sufficient to cover the marzipan. Lift the wire rack and board off the pan and set aside to dry, untouched, for 5 minutes.

14. Return the excess fondant to the double boiler. Gently reheat the fondant and thin it with a tablespoon of water, if necessary. Place the 8-inch tier on a wire rack and set it over the shallow pan. Pour fondant over the tier, spreading it to cover with the spatula. Lift the rack and tier and set aside to dry, untouched, for 5 minutes.

15. Return the excess fondant to the double boiler. Reheat and thin only if necessary. Set the 14-inch tier on a wire rack and coat with fondant. Set aside to dry.

16. Glaze the 10-inch and 6-inch tiers with the remaining fondant and set aside to dry.

17. Using a metal spatula, lift the fondant-covered flakeboard base from its rack and support it on your palm. Trim the excess fondant from the bottom edge with a thin metal spatula, rotating the board as you do so.

18. Trim the bottom of each tier in the same way, 5 to 10 minutes after coating each.

ASSEMBLY & DECORATION

19. Using a ruler, measure the flakeboard base so that the 14-inch tier can be centered on it. Lightly mark the inside of the measure with a toothpick.

20. Supporting the 14-inch tier with a spatula and your hand, carefully center it on the base, withdrawing first your hand and then the spatula as you lower the cake into position.

21. Measure and lightly mark the 14-inch tier to center the 10-inch tier. Measure the height of the 14-inch tier and cut four plastic dowels to this length. Insert the dowels into the bottom of one of the 10-inch plastic separators. Position the separator in the center of the 14-inch cake and press the dowels into the cake until the separator sits directly on the cake's surface. Put a dab of glue in the center of the separator. Place the 10-inch cake, still on its cardboard round, on top of the separator.

22. Measure the height of the 10-inch cake, and cut four dowels to this size. Insert them into the bottom of the 8-inch separator. Attach four 5-inch columns to the top of the separator, fixing them firmly to the four sockets provided. Center the separator on top of the 10-inch cake, pressing the dowels in until the separator sits directly on top of the cake, with the columns extending upward.

23. Place a dab of glue on the second 8-inch separator and put the 8-inch tier, still on its cardboard round, on top. Position this on top of the columns, lining up the tops of the columns with the sockets on the bottom of the separator.

24. Repeat this process for the 6-inch cake, measuring the height of the 8-inch tier to determine the correct length for the dowels, and anchoring the 6-inch tier cardboard base to the second 6-inch separator with glue. At this point, the fully assembled cake may sit at room temperature for 8 to 36 hours before being decorated.

25. To decorate the cake, remove the two top tiers but leave both tiers on their separators. Do not try to remove the columns from the 8- or 10-inch tiers; simply leave them in place as you decorate.

26. Place the flakeboard base and two bottom tiers on a turntable. Using a toothpick, make a tiny mark every 3 inches around the side of the 14-inch tier, about 1 inch from the bottom. At the top of the side (at edge of the bevel), make tiny marks around the rim of the cake, 3 inches apart and falling halfway between each two marks at the lower edge. The marks will help you fill in *V* design of royal icing dots.

27. Spoon royal icing into a pastry bag fitted with a #1 tip or parchment cone with a tiny opening. Starting at one of the higher marks and exerting minimal pressure, pipe a series of delicate comma-shaped lines, reversing every other one, moving diagonally to the lower mark. Keep the lines close together but do not let them run into each other. Continue around the cake until all the *V*s are outlined.

28. Using a little more pressure, and starting at the top of the 14-inch cake where it meets the 10-inch tier, pipe dots around the entire cake, $\frac{1}{8}$ inch apart. Slowly rotate the turntable and hold the bag in the same place, squeezing it in a steady rhythm so that the dots attach to the cake in even rows. The tip of the bag should barely skim the surface of the fondant, and the pressure must pulsate so that the icing is released in spurts, not in a steady flow that would create a line. In the end, the dots should spiral to the outside of the cake.

29. Decorate the 10-inch tier in the same way, beginning the dots at the edge of the separator and working outwards. Decorate the 6- and 8-inch tiers in the same way.

30. Return the flakeboard base and lower tiers to the turntable. Pipe four tiny dots of icing in a diamond pattern in the space between each *V* on the side of the 14-inch tier. With your fingers, carefully pick up a marzipan flower and set it into one dot; complete with three more flowers to form the diamond. Repeat this procedure on all tiers.

31. With the base and lower tiers on the turntable, pipe fine, wispy lines of icing over and around each group of flowers, as in the illustration. Hold the bag lightly and lift it in an arc as you pipe the wisps, so the icing trails from the tip to make a very fine line. Pipe an icing center into each flower. Repeat this procedure with each tier, using the turntable each time.

32. Pipe a design of larger, more elaborate, horizontal commas around the flakeboard base, alternating forward and backward commas. Pipe flourishes around the commas at their tips.

33. With a #3 tip, pipe a shell border of icing around the base of the 14-inch tier. If there is a relatively large gap between the 14- and 10-inch tiers, pipe a shell border around the base of the 10-inch tier. Or, if you prefer, wrap $1\frac{1}{2}$ yards of satin ribbon around the base, piping two dabs of icing halfway around the base to hold the ribbon securely. Tie the ribbon in a small bow and trim the ends.

34. Remove the two bottom tiers and the wooden base from the turntable and set aside at cool room temperature, preferably where the cake is to be served.

35. Place the 8-inch tier on the columns over the 10-inch tier.

36. Carefully position the 6-inch tier on top of the cake. Wrap $1\frac{1}{4}$ yards of ribbon around the base of the 8-inch cake and 1 yard of ribbon around the base of the 6-inch cake. Secure the ribbons with dabs of icing, then tie them into bows.

37. To set the fresh flowers in place, position 1- to 2-inch balls of marzipan or florists' styrofoam on top of the 8- and 10-inch tiers to serve as anchors. Insert the flowers into the anchors until the space between the tiers is filled. Press flowers directly into the top tier or into cut lengths of plastic straw that have been inserted in the cake.

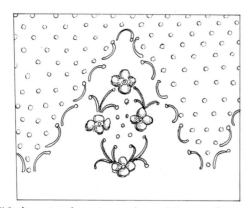

A #1 tip or parchment cone is used in two different ways to create cake design. First, royal icing is piped in alternating comma-shaped lines around cake, using minimal pressure. Next, more pressure is used to create dots around cake, approximately ¼ to ⅛ inch apart, while slowly spinning turntable. Dots and commas are also piped in the center of the V formation and marzipan flowers are glued on using icing dots.

STORING & SERVING

If the cake has to be transported, place the stacked lower tiers and the two smaller tiers in separate boxes, to be assembled where the cake will be served. The decorated cake may sit at room temperature for up to 8 hours before serving. However, the flowers should be added as late as possible.

To serve the cake, remove the 6-inch tier. Discard the flowers and either cut the tier into wedges or reserve for the first anniversary. Lift off the 8-inch tier, remove the separator, dowels, and columns and cut the cake into slices. Serve the lower tiers, removing the separator, dowels, and columns before cutting it into squares and wedges. See the illustrations and information on cutting a wedding cake at the beginning of this chapter.

Sources of Supply

Ateco
August Thomsen Corp.
36 Sea Cliff Avenue
Glen Cove, NY 11542
Equipment; Manufacture and Mail Order

Balducci's
424 Avenue of the Americas
New York, NY 10011
Ingredients; Retail and Mail Order

Bridge Kitchenware Corporation
214 East 52nd Street
New York, NY 10022
Equipment; Manufacture, Retail, and Mail Order

Broadway Panhandler
520 Broadway
New York, NY 10012
Equipment, including H. France crimper; Retail

The Chef's Catalog
3915 Commercial Avenue
Northbrook, IL 60062
Ingredients; Mail Order

Country Kitchen
310 Racquet Drive
Fort Wayne, IN 46825
Equipment; Manufacture, Retail, and Mail Order

Dean & DeLuca
121 Prince Street
New York, NY 10012
Ingredients and Equipment; Retail and Mail Order

Fowler's of Durham
Brightleaf Square
P.O. Box 336
Durham, NC 27701
Ingredients and Equipment; Retail and Mail Order

Kemper Manufacturing
P.O. Box 696
Chino, CA 91710
Equipment; Manufacture and Mail Order

Liberty/Ramsey Imports
Division Universal Foods Corporation
66 Broad Street
Carlstadt, NJ 07072
Ingredients; Mail Order

Maid of Scandinavia
3244 Raleigh Avenue
Minneapolis, MN 55416
Ingredients and Equipment; Retail and Mail Order

Paprikas Weiss Importer
1546 Second Avenue
New York, NY 10028
Ingredients; Retail and Mail Order

Williams-Sonoma
P.O. Box 7456
San Francisco, CA 94120
Equipment; Mail Order

Wilton Enterprises, Inc.
2240 West 75th Street
Woodridge, IL 60517
Ingredients and Equipment; Mail Order

The Bakers

Jane Stacey

Orange Cake with Iced Fruit, Fluted Pound Cake with Berry Puree, Summer Fruit Roulade, Genoise Basket with Raspberries, Dark Chocolate Truffle Cake, Rich Pistachio Cake, Coral Campari Cake, Our Favorite Chocolate Cake, Coffee Praline Cake, Island Coconut Cake, Coffee Creme Brulee, Trompe L'Oeil Slice, Candlelit Cassis Cake, The Chocolate Lover's Birthday Cake, Silly Cupcakes, A Chocolate Valentine, Phi Beta Kappa Cake, Chocolate Fireworks (with Cheryl Kleinman), Harvest Moon Cake, Heartland Thanksgiving Cake, Brandied Christmas Fruitcake, Midnight Yule Log, Lemon Arbor Wedding Cake, Garlands of Flowers Wedding Cakes, and Chocolate Nocturne Wedding Cake.

Ellen Baumwoll

Strawberry Cream Cake, Lemon Rose Cake, Chocolate Cake with Winter Roses, Greatest Hits Cake, Camellia Shower Cake, Heirloom Wedding Cake, and The Lohengrin.

Cheryl Kleinman

Picnic Nut Cake, Strawberry Trifle, Crystal Lemon Cake, Chocolate Galaxy, Miami Casual Cake, Amethyst Buttercream Birthday Cake, Victorian Rosebud Cake, Wild Rose Cake, Starry New Year Cake, Mardi Gras Rum Cake, May Day Dacquoise, Mother's Day Labor of Love, Father's Day Cake, The Halloween Cake, White Chocolate Buche de Noel, Christmas Gold Cake, Porcelain Rose Cake, and Cameo Wedding Cake.

Lisa Cates and Janet Ross

The Giant's Cupcake and The Enchanted Flowerpot.

Prop Credits

COVER: Pine table, Evergreen Antiques; Le Jacquard Francais napkins, Cherchez and Wolfman Good & Gold & Co.; Basket plate (front center) Bardith, Ltd., Copeland plate (right) The English Way, all New York City.

SPRING AND SUMMER: p. 40, Gien tart plate, Barney's New York; p.44, Moustier Lattice plate, Barney's New York; p. 45, Platter, Pottery Barn New York; p. 48, Villeroy & Boch plate and Le Jacquard Francais tablecloth, Barney's New York; p. 49, Thomas Trend platter, Gear Inc. New York; p. 53, Moustier Octagonal plate, Horn cake server, and Le Jacquard Francais tablecloth, Barney's New York.

FALL AND WINTER: p. 56, Plate, The Crystal Shoppe, Perth Amboy, N.J.; p. 61, Pedestal, The Crystal Shoppe, Perth Amboy, N.J.; p. 64, Russel Wright; p. 68, Plate, Viking U.S.A. and cake server, Gear Inc. New York; p. 69, Plate, Gear Inc. New York.

BIRTHDAY CAKES: p. 84, Fiestaware; p. 85, Moustier Octagonal plate, Barney's New York; p. 89, For Apricot Cobbler © 1983, Dorothy Hafner, New York; p. 96, Fiestaware.

BIRTHDAY CAKES: p. 100, Russel Wright; p. 101, Gear Garden/Grazia, Gear Inc. New York; p. 105, Platter, Thaxton's & Co. New York; p. 108, Russel Wright.

HOLIDAY CAKES: p. 112, Clear Viking, Gear Inc. New York; p. 116, Carnival © 1979, Dorothy Hafner, New York; p. 117, Platter, Pottery Barn, New York; p. 120, Gear Garden/Grazia, Gear Inc. New York; p. 125, Clear Viking, Gear Inc. New York and Le Jacquard Francais tablecloth, Barney's New York; p. 136, Platter, Pottery Barn, New York; p. 137. Pedestal, The Crystal Shoppe, Perth Amboy, N.J.; p. 140, Platter, Thaxton's & Co. New York; p. 141, Clear Viking, Gear Inc. New York; p. 144, Platter, Pottery Barn, New York; p. 145, Clear Viking, Gear Inc. New York.

WEDDINGS: p. 153, Tablecloth, The Crystal Shoppe, Perth Amboy, N.J.; p. 164, Platter, Thaxton's & Co. New York.

Index

Entries in *italics* refer to illustrations

ACKNOWLEDGMENTS:

We'd like to thank the following people for their support, encouragement, and long hours of help: Debra Carbarnes; Mary Dauman; Lonnie Danchik; Leonard and Phyllis Dorfman; Sue Ewell; Leslie Fagen; Anne Ferril; Mary Forsell; Sara Jane Foster; Jody Thompson Kennedy; Roberta Kins; Evelyn, Harold, and Jill Kleinman; Joseph Lanciani; Madeline Lanciani; Stephen Morse; Elizabeth Saft; Sarah Stewart; Sarah Tahourdin.